FRANCE

AN ILLUSTRATED HISTORY

FRANCE

AN ILLUSTRATED HISTORY

LISA NEAL

HIPPOCRENE BOOKS, INC.
New York

944
NEA
2991610

Some photos herein courtesy of Tor Eigeland.

ISBN 0-7818-0835-9 (hardcover)
ISBN 0-7818-0872-3 (paperback)

For information, address:
HIPPOCRENE BOOKS, INC.
171 Madison Avenue
New York, NY 10016

Cataloging-in-Publication Data available from the Library of Congress.

Printed in the United States of America.

TABLE OF CONTENTS

INTRODUCTION: FRENCH HISTORIES

The task of writing a broad history of France is daunting and humbling. I have tried to write a history that is intelligible to a general audience, a history of the kind I myself would want to read. When I focus on significant historical events, I emphasize the effects they had on French urban and rural communities. In each period, I have delved into the life of at least one important person in an effort to give each era a human face. When information about domestic life—and in particular the roles women played and sometimes appropriated for themselves in society—is available and reliable, I have included it, and have tried to broaden my view beyond Paris, on which traditional political histories tend to focus. Finally, I have looked to French literature to provide insights into the past.

Each chapter of this book covers one era of French history, from prehistoric times to the present day. Certain themes recur: the relations of France with its neighbors, the ever-present tension within France between national unity and regional autonomy, the role of the Church, and developments in public works and education.

Napoleon defined history as "the version of past events that people have decided to agree upon," but he did not specify *which*

1

people, or *whose* version. The historian must choose not only which events to study, but also which perception or perceptions of a given event to include. This is particularly difficult in the case of France.

French history—perhaps more than many national histories—is a kind of work in progress, because the French are continually rereading and rewriting it. For example, the French Revolution of 1789 still sparks hot debates, almost as if it occurred recently. In a sense, such an event is as recent as the last re-evaluation of it. Just this week, the front page of a French national newspaper, *Le Monde*, featured an analysis of the French Revolution entitled, "Ma Révolution Préférée" ("My Favorite Revolution"). The French cannot rid themselves of their history; it permeates their world, enriching and tormenting their lives with never-to-be resolved questions.

The author of a history of France must take into account the ways in which the French have viewed these questions over time: their historical self-representation. In France, such representation takes place on the level of popular culture as well as in academic circles; both bookstores and university libraries abound in texts treating historical topics from every imaginable angle. A visitor to France cannot help but take notice of the plethora of popular periodicals, novels, films, and documentaries dealing with French history. An entire television channel exclusively shows historically oriented programs. Historical events, and the approaches used to study them, fall into and out of favor almost as fast as Parisian *haute couture*.

To complicate matters further, each region represents itself differently. Joan of Arc is more vitally present in the minds and imagination of the northern French than of the southern. Southerners are more inclined to glorify the Cathars, medieval heretics who resisted the authority and hegemony of the Catholic Church, which, by the way, was administered from centers in the *north*. Even within each region, individual cities have their own favorite historical figures whose names adorn parks, streets, and school—to a greater extent, I believe, than in other Western countries. Many a French child lives on a street whose name is a famous person or an historical date. Even toll roads in the different parts of France reflect, on the brown signs we all speed past, the differing self-representations of each region.

For over twenty years, I have observed the French preoccupation with history at close hand—through frequent visits and now permanent residence—but also at a certain remove because I am an American. My first awareness of the primordial place that history occupies for the French occurred in the 1970s when I guided groups of French and American teenagers on bicycle trips through the Loire Valley and Burgundy—two regions particularly rich in architectural history. The French youths were familiar with the various kings and castles and were clearly proud to show their patrimony to their American friends, though at times they seemed blasé when confronted with yet another remarkably beautiful Renaissance castle. The young Americans, on the other hand, were often awed by the splendor of the castles and the romantic and sometimes grisly stories told about their original occupants. At the end of the day, however, the Americans were often unable to date the castles within three centuries of their construction.

Sign along a highway near Béziers, in southern France, drawing attention to the historical role played by the Cathars, a twelfth-century religious sect.

In the train station of a relatively small town (50,000 inhabitants), several shelves in the newstand are devoted exclusively to books and periodicals dealing with historical topics.

Like my young American compatriots, I have also experienced such uninformed enthusiasm. Once, I came upon a segment of an ancient road, the Via Domitia, while climbing a bluff in south-central France. I had searched for the road elsewhere to no avail, and then, suddenly, found it where I had not expected it. The irregularly shaped, but still intact paving stones stretched out for a kilometer before me. Tears came to my eyes. To think I was standing on the very stones laid there by the Romans! Only while doing research for this book, did I discover that the Romans did *not* originally build the great road, but rather the Gauls before them.

Would a French person of my age and education have made this error? It is hard to say, but one thing is certain: my French students on the bicycle trip had a more fully developed and precise sense of French history than I had of American or world history when I was their age. There was nothing exceptional about these students; a sense of history seems to be a part of the French national character. One could explain this simply by noting that most people living in France confront vestiges from bygone eras daily, from street signs to Gothic churches. Contemporary and ancient buildings share space, just as the present shares space with the past in the French mind.

An even more compelling factor in the heightened sense of history in France, however, is the treatment of history in French schools. (Education has been compulsory and free since the nineteenth century.) Thus, a French-educated person—like my own American-born daughter—receives a state-endorsed image of the history of the country.

One quick example: in the first years of the Third Republic (1875–1940), the French salved the pain of their disastrous

6

Vestiges of this Roman road, the "Via Domitia," remain throughout southern France.

defeat by the Prussians in 1870 by presenting the Gallic leader, Vercingétorix—himself defeated by the Romans in 52 B.C.—in a posture of patriotic grandeur. In a painting reproduced in countless French textbooks since the late nineteenth century, we see the defiant Gaul laying his weapons at Caesar's feet. Textbooks often fail to point out the lack of historical accuracy in the depiction of the weapons, and omit the fact that Vercingétorix was executed six years later in Rome. The point of showing school children the painting is not so much to convey a historically accurate representation of an event, as to foster in them a sense of belonging to a noble lineage.

To this particularly nineteenth-century version of a moment in French history, one could add revisions and additions from other sources and historical periods. In fact, a book the size of the one you are now holding could be filled with nothing but interpretations of the Roman conquest of Gaul (which some historians might be loathe to call a conquest at all!). To make a readable history, I have focused on certain characters and anecdotes because, quite simply, I find them intriguing. (The French word, *histoire,* means both history and story; *intrigue* refers to something arousing our interest but it also means *plot*.) I hope readers will share my fascination with the twists and turns of the French story.

In a scene familiar to all French students, Vercingétorix, leader of the Gauls, defiantly throws his arms at the feet of the victor, Julius Caesar.

CHAPTER ONE

GAUL: FROM CAVES TO VILLAS

Prehistory

France has been inhabited for almost two million years, though the actual record of man's presence begins considerably later. A hundred thousand years ago, Neanderthal man weathered the harsh conditions of his era, and his remains have been found at several sites in France. Neanderthal man was advanced enough to bury his dead and even to place beside the deceased offerings of tools or flowers (though some experts now believe the scattered human bones found in Neanderthal caves are proof of cannibalism).

France is a veritable treasure trove for paleontologists. In 1971, the complete front section of the skull of a man who lived 450,000 years ago was discovered in Tautavel, near Perpignan. First excavated in 1828, the site is now world famous and possesses a very technologically sophisticated museum with numerous reconstructions of prehistoric man and his environment. The extraordinary number of bones and stone tools found in the area provide evidence of human habitation over many centuries. At the time "Tautavel man" lived, fire had not yet been discovered and tools were rudimentary. With nothing but crude wooden spears, these early nomadic hunters tackled mammals as large as modern wolves and bison. They appeared to live in groups of about twenty, but we still know little about their dwellings.

Skeletons of a more "modern" man were discovered in 1868 at Cro-Magnon, near Les Eyzies in Dordogne. Classified as *Homo sapiens sapiens*, Cro-Magnon Man appeared in Western Europe about 35,000 years ago. He is our direct ancestor, either following Neanderthal man after the latter died out or, some claim, coexisting with him for up to five thousand years. This era marks the beginning of art, at least as we know it. These early men decorated everyday objects and portrayed humans on rocks, as well as creating jewelry and statuettes.

An exceptionally rich example of prehistoric art was discovered in the fall of 1940 by four children playing near a cave outside of Lascaux (Dordogne). Although the world had other pressing problems that year—France had fallen to Germany three months earlier—the discovery captivated the imagination of the Western world and changed our thinking about early man and the ways he lived and expressed himself. The monumental paintings cover some twenty chambers and depict thousands of animal figures, and at least one human figure with a bird's head, which are either painted or engraved on the walls of the caverns. All the drawings are executed in a similar style and are thought to date from the thirteenth millennium B.C.

Another fortuitous archeological discovery was made in an Alpine glacier in 1991. There, below the ice, was an intact skeleton from around 5000 B.C., complete with clothes and accessories—a fur cap and necklace—and the copper and stone weapons that the man, now dubbed "Otzi," was carrying. Like earlier discoveries, the skeleton from the Alps greatly contributed to our vision of prehistoric man. "Otzi" had a metal weapon; he was clearly hunting when he met his end.

During the following millennium, people started simple farming. This is the period in which huge menhirs and dolmens were erected in Western Europe and the British Isles. The underlying principle of these megalithic monuments is still a matter of debate, but they share some architectural features and magical symbols, suggesting that they reflect a certain unity of belief. Menhirs were upright stones of great size (the word menhir comes from Breton *men*, "stone," and *hir*, "long") that were placed in circles or semicircles, or in several parallel rows, called alignments. The most famous alignments are in Carnac (Brittany) and include 2,935 menhirs that were probably used for religious rituals. Dolmens, upright supports covered with a large stone roof, vary in shape from region to region, but seem always associated with burial.

Early Gaul

Not until well into the second millennium B.C., however, can we begin to form a more detailed and documented notion of the patterns of settlement in France. Between 1500 and 1300 B.C., at first slowly and then more rapidly, Celtic tribes began to move westward from southern Germany. This migration led to the establishment of Celtic settlements in large portions of present-day France. Between 1200 and 900 B.C., ways of fertilizing and plowing the land were developed, leading to a significant shift toward a more sedentary existence. There followed a period of

Dolmen near Font-Romeu in the Pyrenees. Human remains have frequently been found under intact dolmens.

relative stability. At this point, the territory we now refer to as Gaul was bordered by the Rhine, the Mediterranean, the Pyrenees, and the Atlantic; it was the largest Celtic territory in Antiquity. However, the Celts themselves were in the majority only in the northwest third of this expanse. Other populations lived elsewhere, sometimes on the precise sites that their Neolithic ancestors had inhabited thousands of years before.

Near the end of the sixth century and through the fifth, the Gallic Celts were again on the move, this time toward northern Italy, into the Massif Central and Languedoc. What kind of people were the early Celts and Gauls? Although we have nothing as revealing of their character as personal memoirs, archeological evidence tells us much. Iron weapons, the result of advances in metallurgy in the seventh century B.C., suggest that new modes of warfare and social organization were then appearing. Warriors in Gaul were becoming a noble class, much like the one later encountered in medieval feudalism; they dominated political life and formed new alliances among peoples.

Gauls and Greeks

Concurrently, an important shift in trading practices was leading to increased openness toward foreigners and the adoption of new habits. Gaul began to trade with its Mediterranean neighbors—Greece, Rhodes, and Spain—both by water and land. It was the Greeks who founded Marseille around 600 B.C. as a maritime trading center. As previously mentioned, the Gauls were responsible for building an important roadway, the Via Domitia, linking

Italy and Spain, as well as numerous other thoroughfares used by merchants and soldiers.

The vestiges of this era bear testimony to the extent of the commercial exchanges between Gaul and the Mediterranean, Greek-dominated world. Archeologists have uncovered articles and coins from numerous distant lands, some predating the founding of Marseille. For instance, Etruscan and Rhodian articles have been found near Saint Blaise and Colmar, and Ionian and Rhodian articles in Alsace.

Many of the cities dating from this period are still thriving today, such as Nice, Antibes, Agde, and Arles. Founded as trading centers, these cities still display with pride the vestiges of their early history, though the Greek influence has been somewhat obscured by the more enduring monuments from the era of Roman rule, many of which were themselves inspired by the Greek esthetic. The Maison Carrée (Square House) in Nimes, for example, displays the balance and purity of line that characterizes Greek architecture. This structure inspired Thomas Jefferson as he planned the capital of Virginia.

Smaller, more provincial settlements, called *oppida*, were also built. Some of these were abandoned under the Romans, however, and most of the others did not survive long into the Middle Ages. For reasons of defense, the Gallic *oppida* were usually located on plateaus surrounded by ditches and terraces. Though more rustic than the cities, the *oppida* were nonetheless cosmopolitan insofar as they were exposed to and certainly benefited from the visits of merchants who crisscrossed the land along the various trade routes. Such would be the case of the *Oppidum* du Mont Lassois (in Vix, Côte-d'Or), which, inhabited

The ruins of an oppidum, a Gallic village, built on a plateau for defense (and in this picture serving as a playground for the author's daughter).

as early as the sixth century B.C. and well into the Gallo-Roman era, was probably a major way station for tin going from Cornwall to Italy or Greece along the Rhone Valley. It may also have served as a point for commercial exchange with the east of France and present-day Switzerland. Other *oppida* that served the trade routes are located in the Jura, in southern Germany, and in southeastern France.

The geographical extent of Greek influence in pre-Roman Gaul is truly astounding. As far from the Mediterranean as Normandy, Lorraine, and Alsace, artifacts and coins bearing Greek motifs and writing have been discovered. In fact, before the advent of Latin in the first century B.C., the Celts used Greek characters for writing their own language. Linguists claim that throughout present-day France many local dialects contain words of Greek origin.

When the Greeks founded Marseille in 600 B.C., the local populations melded easily with them. This situation changed around 400 B.C. when new waves of northerners moved southward toward Italy, eventually sacking Rome in 390 B.C. It was the Romans who coined the term, "Gaul," for these invaders whom they considered "barbarians." The Romans referred to the land from which the Gallic tribes came as "Gallia Comata," or "Long-haired Gaul"; and they mocked the Gauls as impetuous drunkards. But the truth was that a sizeable portion of Gaul was quite highly civilized—especially the southern areas covered, ironically, with the vineyards that the Romans would later develop further to satisfy their own taste for wine.

It was this part of Gaul that, between 181 and 125 B.C., felt compelled to appeal to Rome in order to defend itself from the "barbarian" tribes. This was a primary factor in the eventual conquest of all of Gaul by Rome. Southern Gaul—Greek Gaul—*requested* the presence of the highly trained and efficient Roman armies to protect the commercial exchanges that formed the basis of the economy in that region. As it happened, Rome was then pursuing expansionist policies, and was all too happy to do the Greeks' bidding! Motivating them too was the recollection of having suffered a humiliation at the hands of Gallic warriors two hundred years earlier.

In 125 B.C., the Romans annexed Southern Gaul—an area that stretched from the Mediterranean to Lake Geneva—calling it first *Provincia* and later *Narbonensis,* after its capital Narbonne. The rest of Gaul remained independent for seventy more years, until Julius Caesar went on his famous military campaign. Six years later, in 52 B.C., Caesar conquered the last rebellious Gallic tribe at Alesia—a defeat celebrated and immortalized in Royer's nineteenth-century painting (page 9).

Roman Gaul

In a relatively short time, Gaul was transformed. How did this happen? The answer provides insight into the social hierarchy in Gaul, as well as into the principles guiding the Romans as they moved into the conquered land. The first thing to keep in mind is that only a few hundred Romans administrators were sent to oversee a population estimated at around ten million. Most of the high-level administrative tasks were thus performed by Gauls from among members of the upper (military) and merchant classes. There is little doubt that these classes, as well as landowners, prospered under the Roman regime. Many peasants, however, viewed the advent of the Romans with less enthusiasm. Certain Gallic towns shared the mistrustful and even resistant attitude that characterized most of the peasant class. Revolts against the Romans occurred in 21 and 69–70 A.D., but they were easily suppressed. There was more to gain by accommodating the Romans than by resisting them.

As the "Pax Romana" continued, the competition among Gallo-Roman cities had to do not with militarization but rather with how willingly the city adopted Roman ways of life and language. In a few decades, Latin had already made inroads in education, administration, and in commercial exchanges throughout Gaul—in places where the Greek language had never ventured. Gallic cities were categorized in function of the extent to which they had initially accepted the Roman victory. An individual's rights and his status under the law were determined in large part by the status of the city and region where he lived. Of the four large regions comprising greater Gaul, *Narbonensis* enjoyed a more privileged position due to its longstanding interactions with the Greeks and Romans. To this province went retired Roman soldiers, *coloniae*, transforming it into a land of city-states. The other three Gauls—*Belgica*, *Lugdunum* (Lyons), and *Aquitania*—were made up of *civitates* corresponding roughly to the different tribes and peoples who inhabited the region. Romans nonetheless controlled the *civitates*, each of which had its own capital.

A Country under Construction

If Gaul was quickly Romanized, this was due in no small part to the implicit attitude of Romans toward the "vanquished." Rome saw that it was not in its interests to subjugate and over-tax the Gauls. A prosperous Gaul made better business sense than a broken land and people. The Romans did require that the Gauls pay property taxes, but they improved the infrastructure of Greater Gaul at the same time, adding considerably to the existing roads and waterways, and building the amazing aqueducts for which they are renowned. To give an idea of the magnitude of their water management system: Lyon, the capital of high imperial Gaul, was supplied with around seventy-five cubic meters of water per day. To accomplish this feat, four aqueducts were built over a distance of two hundred kilometers. The water ran in pipes made of lead, brick, or wood and was stored in large reservoirs or distributed from public fountains. The more privileged city residents enjoyed running water in their own homes. Lyon was no exception; ruins of luxurious private homes containing a *tepidarium* (a Roman bath) have been discovered throughout Roman Gaul, for example, in Autun (Burgundy) and in Kervenennec en Pont-Croix (Brittany). Other public works and buildings built under Roman rule included theaters, stadiums, public markets, prisons, baths, temples, and libraries. Occasionally, the precise function of a given building is today a matter of debate. The building referred to as the "Temple of Diane" in Nimes, for example, may very well have been a public library, rather than a religious site as was long thought.

The rate of construction in Roman Gaul was prodigious. Existing Gallic cities were often greatly expanded and Romanized—for

Remains of a Roman bridge on the Via Domitia.

The Temple of Diana and the "Maison Carrée" (below), built in the 2nd century A.D. The "Temple de Diane" remained intact until 1562, but is today in ruins.

The Pont du Gard was part of a Roman aqueduct that carried water over hundreds of kilometers.

This arena was built during the reign of the Flavians (69–96) at Arles, a city that was an important commercial center even before the arrival of the Romans in Gaul.

instance, Besançon and the *oppidum* of Biturgies—and many cities were built from the ground up, including Amiens, Carhaix, Limoges, and Autun. A great deal of planning went into these projects; a grid was laid and streets were plotted at right angles. Motorists in present-day France might be surprised to learn that the Gallo-Romans organized their streets so that traffic could flow into the heart of the city, the *forum*, a large open square surrounded by shops and walkways. To facilitate traffic, streets were paved in stone or graveled, reaching a width of four to six meters, and cambered so that rain ran into the gutters. Sidewalks were also wide, and for the most part covered with a roof resting on columns.

Among all the public buildings erected in the first hundred years of Roman rule, those designed for entertainment are perhaps the most well known. Some, like a theater in Orange and the arenas in Nimes and Arles, are again being used for their original purposes. (Rather than gladiators, the arena in Nimes now welcomes bullfighters!) In building these structures, especially the huge amphitheaters, cities incurred great costs that could not be covered by tax revenues alone; wealthy citizens and leaders from outside the city were called upon to contribute. The theater in Orange, the best preserved from the entire Roman Empire, was clearly bankrolled by the Emperor Augustus, a statue of whom looks down on center stage.

Augustus was responsible for the first theaters in Roman Gaul, built near the end of the first century B.C. It was, however, during the reign of the Flavians (69–96 A.D.) that the pace of building in Roman Gaul accelerated, and continued well into the second century. Rome was not built in a day, and neither was

Roman Gaul. The first of the Roman provinces, *Narbonensis* benefited earlier, and more consistently, from the zeal to recast the country in Rome's image. Other areas of Gaul were transformed, to be sure, but as time went on they also were more subject to border strife.

Under the late Roman Empire (250–400 A.D.) two Germanic tribes—the Alemanni and the Franks—began to prey upon their Gallic neighbors. During this time, eastern and northern cities began a program of fortification, surrounding themselves with towering stone walls, some of which are still visible today. This marks the beginning of a significant shift in certain areas of Gaul. Whereas cities had previously depended upon Roman law and the Roman legions to maintain order, henceforth Gauls in the borderlands had to prepare themselves against the ever-present threat of attack. The central authority provided by the Empire was on the wane.

The Empire did not, of course, end in the third century. Though Roman Gaul experienced economic crises and military setbacks in that era, not all aspects of life came to a standstill. Long renowned in Gaul, higher education continued to flourish in the late third and fourth centuries. Gaul could boast of several famous universities, and educated Gauls took their place in Roman imperial administration with a greater frequency than they had in the first century of Roman rule. To give but one notable example: Ausonius (310–393), who taught at the University of Bordeaux, was appointed as the tutor of the future emperor Gratian. By the mid-fourth century, Christianity was gaining a foothold in Gaul. Monasticism, introduced by Martin de Tours (*c.* 316–397), provided a means by which young Gäuls could be educated. More importantly, perhaps, Christianity offered an organizing principle in areas of Gaul where Roman authority was being eroded.

Everyday Life in Gaul

Through the five hundred years of Roman presence in Gaul, the great majority of people (over 90% by one estimate) lived on the land. One of the first acts of Emperor Augustus after the Roman conquest was to organize a land register in order to collect taxes. Parcels were plotted as fifty hectare squares (one hectare is about 2.5 acres). The best parcels of land were given to war veterans, the *coloniae*, and exempted from tax; others were rented to peasants, and still others remained state property. Farms were run both by Roman colonists and by Gauls, with paid laborers and slaves often living on the premises.

Pliny the Elder (23–79 A.D.) wrote that his Roman compatriots were impressed by the Gauls' agricultural skill. Plows, reapers, and forged sickles had long been in common use, and the Gauls had also mastered the arts of fertilization and soil enrichment. Cereals had been grown throughout Gaul for centuries and, as previously mentioned, grapes had been long cultivated in the *Narbonensis*. The Romans encouraged wine production in the Bordeaux region in the first century A.D.; by the fourth century, vines were being cultivated around Paris and on the Moselle and the Rhine. In fact, the Italians at one point became worried about competing with Gallic wine. Consequently, the Roman emperor ordered the destruction of vast vineyards in Gaul. Fortunately, his orders were not followed!

The most common country residence was the "villa," comprising both a home for the landowner (*pars urbana*) and utilitarian structures for farming (*pars agraria*). The size and style of these buildings varied greatly from one region of Roman Gaul to another. Some villas from this era were simply added onto existing Gallic residences, like the ruins found at Etoile-la-Tranquille in the Somme and the "villa de Mayen" in the Rhine Valley. It appears that villas were constructed according to the same techniques used in urban public structures: masonry walls with mortar, tiles, and even heating for private *thermes*. There was often great attention given to interior decoration: mural paintings, sculpture, and mosaics.

Farmers who rented land did not live in villas but rather in "vici," small settlements in which local markets were held. Some vici were large enough to constitute veritable cultural centers containing public baths, a sanctuary, and perhaps a theater. Of the sixty or so small theaters in Gaul dating from the first centuries of Roman rule, at least half are located in towns of secondary importance or in the countryside itself. Rather than the tragedies and comedies that were commonly shown in Rome and perhaps in the larger Gallo-Roman cities, the country theaters were more apt to stage pantomime, dance, and farces in which more emphasis was placed on choreography and set design than on the script.

Public baths were not only places to wash but also centers for relaxation, much like present-day European spas—with the difference that the Gallo-Roman baths were generally free or moderately priced. Men and women were admitted separately according to set schedules. The leisure activities at the baths included physical exercises, reading, conversation, music, massage, and, of course, swimming.

Much information about the appearance of Gauls, their environment, and their everyday life can be gleaned from burial sites. From the scenes sculpted on sarcophagi and the objects buried along with the deceased, we can see how the Roman Gauls were clothed: short belted tunics, and longer tunics for women, with a woolen cape (*sagum*) or a more voluminous hooded cape (*cucullus*) to protect from inclement weather. Since the bas-reliefs sometimes depict entire rooms, we can also see the style of furniture in vogue through the centuries. In addition, values such as motherhood and conjugal devotion are reflected in the chiseled stone.

Gallic Religion and Rites

Since the early Gauls and Celts left little written information about their religion, perhaps because of their reverence for the art of memory, our knowledge of it is based on inscriptions on statuary, in particular funeral monuments, and the writings of the Greeks and Romans. When the Romans first arrived in greater Gaul, the Gauls were practicing a kind of polytheism as compatible with Roman mythology as it had been with Greek. Gallic gods with Greek and Roman equivalents were simply transformed. The Greeks thus identified the god Lugus (or Lug) as the sun god Apollo. Caesar, on the other hand, associated this Gallic god with Mercury, because of his ubiquity: "The god they most venerate is Mercury," wrote Caesar in one of his seven volumes on the Gallic War. Occasionally, a transformed Gallic god remained clothed in traditional Gallic garb and carried a

Gallic epithet like "Apollo-Borvo." Borvo was the Gallic god of healing water, which later gave rise to the French royal name "Bourbon"—and, of course, the famous American healing water from Kentucky. The faithful came to be healed at Bourbonne-les-Bains, for example, where the plaques sculpted to thank Apollo-Borvo are inscribed with images of the formerly ailing body parts.

Does the melding of the identities of Roman and Gallic deities mean that there was a corresponding transformation of the two belief systems? Experts tend to think not. This is perhaps not surprising; the Gallic spirit of animism and dreamlike consciousness was fundamentally different from the "state religion" of Rome. Celtic and Gallic myths contain stories of metamorphosis, woodland rituals, and magic bonds between humans and animals. Certain types of wood are considered sacred; the name "Druid" comes in fact from an ancient Indo-European word associating knowledge and the oak tree. Hills were believed to be guarded by spirits, often female, some of whose names are still used.

From the second century onward, there was a resurgence of archaic Celtic and Gallic symbols and gods that had no clear equivalent in Roman religion. One such god was Cernunnos, whose images have been found as far south as Italy—under Celtic occupation at the date of the image (400 B.C.)—and as far north as Denmark, on a silver ritual vessel dating from the first century B.C. Cernunnos, this well traveled and widely known Gallic deity, was considered the lord of all wild things. He is normally depicted wearing stag antlers or accompanied by a stag and a ram-horned serpent. He was still powerful enough in the era of early Christianity to be opposed by Christians. In fact,

Cernunnos' image appears in medieval manuscripts as the embodiment of the Antichrist.

Just as Christians and Gallic pagans often viewed the same god in mutually exclusive ways, so did the Romans and Gauls interpret some of the same legends differently. The Roman historian Livy (c. 60 B.C.–17 A.D.), for example, recounts another tale concerning a stag. The story derives from the Battle of Sentinum (295 B.C.), where the current adversaries of Rome, the Samnites, had persuaded the Gauls to join with them and form a coalition strong enough to prevail against the Romans. At the height of this battle, a deer pursued by a wolf broke onto the battlefield and ran toward the Gauls, who showered it with deadly arrows. The wolf found refuge among the Romans. The Gauls interpreted the death of the deer as a sacrifice (which indeed was a common ritual in their religion) that assured their immediate victory. The Romans, on the other hand, saw in the wolf an embodiment of Mars—the god of war who guaranteed their ultimate victory (which did indeed occur some years later).

Tales such as this one, written by a contemporary, are a good source of information about the legends that informed Gallic religion. Unfortunately, few such tales have come down to us, except in the writings of Poseidonius, Lucan, Livy, and Julius Caesar. In a recent archeological dig at a burial site, however, tangible evidence of stag sacrifice was found: a domesticated stag, complete with iron bit, was found lying in the grave of a Gallic warrior. This animal was probably sacrificed to ensure the immortality of the deceased. According to the Roman poet and historian, Lucan (39–65 A.D.), the Gauls also practiced human sacrifice, though there is little if any archeological evidence to support his claim.

It is clear that the Gauls believed strongly in the transmigration of souls. The otherworld was conceived as an island or islands whose inhabitants enjoyed eternal youth, frolicking, singing, and engaging in military contests. Religious rites were conducted in a variety of milieus. Public sanctuaries were often constructed on mountains, at crossroads, and at water sources, much like Christian shrines in a later age. In addition to such public temples of particular gods, to which pilgrimages were made, there were private altars in Gallic-Roman homes. Religious rites also took place in the open, though we know little about them. It is clear that there were set funeral rituals. Up until the end of the second century, bodies were cremated and the ashes put into an urn and buried along with symbolic objects, such as the sacrificed stag. Most burial sites were outside the main living area of towns and *oppida*; they were often located alongside roads, so travelers could read the epitaphs.

The End of Roman Gaul

We have been able to glean so much information from funeral monuments largely because they were later used, and thus preserved, as building blocks for defensive ramparts built to protect cities, *oppida,* and private villas. During the tumultuous third century, when marauders roamed the land, Gauls were anxious to protect themselves with walls. Other invaders appeared on the scene in the fifth century—notably the Visigoths—and again, fortification was the response. The end of Roman Gaul did not happen with a bang; there were sporadic periods of peace and prosperity in the years before the final collapse of the Empire.

The Franks and Burgundians had, by 418, established themselves west of the Rhine in territory formerly held by the Romans; the Visigoths, for their part, had settled in *Aquitania*. There are few indications, however, that the Gauls ever attempted to sever their long-standing relationship with the Roman Empire, though they had ample opportunity to do so as the fifth century progressed. On the contrary, the Gauls continued to look to Rome for protection and guidance until the last Roman possessions in Gaul were ceded to the Visigoths in 476 A.D. This is the fateful date—the last sacking of Rome—that marks the definitive end of Roman Gaul.

CHAPTER TWO

THE MIDDLE AGES THROUGH THE THIRTEENTH CENTURY

Overview: From Legends to Reality (and Back)

In the modern mind, the Middle Ages conjure up images of King Arthur's round table, dragon-slaying crusaders in shining armor, roaming minstrels singing of noble ladies and love, and castles with turrets and moats. Indeed, with the exception of the dragons, all these existed during the nearly ten centuries we now call the Middle Ages.

The world of the Middle Ages is the stuff of legend, but it is also shaped *by* legend. The medieval legends we still recount were also known to medieval people, and therefore provided them with models of behavior to emulate or avoid. Many legends were conveyed by word of mouth for centuries before being scratched onto parchment. The Arthurian legends, common to both England and France, were part of the oral tradition from about the sixth century, but were first written down in the early twelfth century by Geoffrey of Monmouth, who may have been of Breton descent. In Monmouth's *Historia regum Britanniae,* the illustrious King Arthur defeats a Roman army. Arthur is the good king, the story tells us, who conceived of a round table to foster equality among his faithful knights—but he is mortally wounded in a rebellion led by his nephew. Here we see several of the pressing preoccupations of the medieval world, both literary and literal: valor, loyalty, and betrayal.

Some written legends took as their basis documented historical events—for example, the "Song of Roland," an epic poem that immortalizes the exodus of Charlemagne's troops from Spain in 778. The poem, written some three hundred years after the historical battle, reflects the early twelfth century's tendency to demonize Moslems in order to glorify the ongoing battle against them. (In the real battle, the adversaries of the Christians were not Moslems, but Basques, and the battle was a mere skirmish.) In a sense, the poem served as an agent of propaganda to foster enthusiasm for crusades to the Holy Land.

The poem also reveals two slightly different conceptions of medieval valor, the many faces of betrayal, and a feminine form of chivalric fidelity. Roland embodies one kind of valor: the preoccupation with glory on the battlefield above all else. Another character in the poem, Olivier, beseeches Roland to summon help from Charlemagne by sounding his horn. Olivier is faithfully committed to his military purpose, but he displays an instinct for survival. Such pragmatism, when it manifests itself without dishonor, is as much an aspect of feudal chivalry as Roland's single-minded quest for glory.

The betrayals in the "Song of Roland" are perpetrated by the Moslems (or Saracens), who in Christian representations are never to be trusted, as well as by Roland's evil step-father, Ganelon, who conspires with the Saracens. Blood ties are far from infrangible, as will be seen in the ever-changing alliances of the

A scene from The Song of Roland.

French royal houses. One can be betrayed from without (the foreign Other), but also from within (the family).

When Roland's betrothed learns of his death, she immediately dies of shock and chagrin. For her there are no moderate measures; she is the female equivalent of Roland in her unyielding fidelity to her beliefs. She is faithful to love, he to glory. The treacherous Ganelon suffers death, and the medieval world order is thus restored, though at a tragic price.

Other legends highlight prowess in love more than on the battlefield. These legends are the courtly love poems in which a knight-lover lives in order to serve—in fact, to *worship*—his invariably aristocratic and married Lady. These lyrical poems first appeared in the eleventh century and were sung by troubadours across the south of France. Courtly love is compatible with and complements the more militaristic legends; though in the tales of love, the object of fidelity is less the king (or military glory) than the lady, or rather love itself. Among the milieus favorable to the production and performance of courtly love poetry in the eleventh and twelfth centuries were the courts of Queen Eleanor of Aquitaine (Aliénor in French) and her daughter Marie de Champagne. The revolution of thought and sentiment associated with courtly love affected not only later centuries, but also the age in which it was written. These were legends in their own time and, as such, played formative roles in the medieval imagination.

However, these effects should not be exaggerated. Loyalty—whether to a seigneur, to the ideal of glory, or to a lady—was difficult to maintain in the face of harsh realities. The relationship between lord and liege was financial and military more than spiritual: knights owed their overlords a certain number of days of service per year in return for their overlords' protection. Since these overlords—from minor barons to great kings—had no standing armies, soldiers had to be assembled for each battle, or rather for each battle "season," beginning after Lent and running through the summer. Medieval warfare was much like baseball: a seasonal sport whose players engaged in training and other unrelated activities during a good part of the time and were called onto the field only for a specific period of the year. When knights had fulfilled their required time, mercenary soldiers had to be hired if the warfare had not yet been brought to a decisive conclusion. By the fourteenth century, roaming bands of unemployed mercenary soldiers often pillaged the very villages, laid waste to the very lands, and raped the very women, they had recently been paid to protect. The rules of chivalry extolled in epic poetry were meaningless to these brigands, who constituted a serious threat to royal power in certain areas.

The ideal of loyalty to one's lady was probably even more difficult to realize in the medieval world than fidelity to one's seigneur. The Middle Ages did not provide a context in which romantic love as we know it could easily develop. For one thing, the Church clearly opposed adultery—or any pleasures of the flesh, for that matter. (For centuries, spouses were discouraged from displaying or even feeling physical desire for one other.) Noble ladies of the kind revered in poems of courtly love were considered property to be disposed of at the discretion of their fathers and husbands. Young noble women with substantial dowries (normally real estate) generally had very little to say about whom they married or, once married, the kind of company they could keep in their new homes. Marriage was a business relationship with the potential to blend estates and calm feudal feuds. A medieval woman was less likely to perish, as did Roland's beloved—for love—than she was to succumb to the black plague, errant brigands, or even irate husbands. The stereotype of medieval damsels locked away for years in towers has indisputable historical bases. Eleanor of Aquitaine, herself the object of a husband's ire, spent over a decade sequestered in the grim Tower of Salisbury, far from the courtly love poetry of her cherished Southwestern France.

The Early Middle Ages (500–1000 A.D.)

But let us back up. We have been evoking images and events belonging to the twelfth and fourteenth centuries, hundreds of years after the departure of the Romans from Gaul. What happened in those intervening years?

Although historians now reject the oversimplification implicit in the term "Dark Ages," the first five hundred years after the fall of the Roman Empire could be rightly called "somber": warfare was a constant, cities were abandoned and fell into ruins, commerce slowed, and the centers of learning the Gauls had created disappeared, along with much of the culture they had produced and transmitted.

This decline on multiple levels has long been associated with the early fifth-century arrival of various ethnic groups, mostly Germanic (Teutonic) and Viking, referred to as "barbarians." Some modern historians note the fundamental antagonism between the immigrant groups and the Romanized Gauls already established in France, and argue that the barbarians put an end to most vestiges of high culture, from political and economic structures to intellectual and artistic milieus. Others, however, point out that Gaul had already declined considerably by the time the Roman Empire ended, and try to show how the "barbarian" newcomers created a new order. A third answer to the question of barbarian integration in early medieval Gaul takes into account the significant social, political, and cultural differences that existed within France at this time. In the southern areas penetrated by Teutonic groups, many social and political structures from the Roman era had been maintained, though they were perhaps weaker than they had been in the high Roman Empire. In northern Gaul, which had never been as completely Romanized, the immigrant newcomers had a much freer hand in establishing their own social structures.

There is no definitive answer to the question of whether the barbarians clashed, or rather fused, with Gallic culture. Clashes occurred, to be sure, but a great fusion of peoples—in some cases, encouraged by the immigrants—also took place during this time. For example, certain ethnic groups allowed and fostered mixed marriages—whereas the Romans had outlawed them—and accepted men from outside their clan into their armies. Generations of different migrants settled in France, which was considered the western frontier of civilization. These immigrants formed a variegated group, something like a series of geologic strata. Over these five hundred years, a number of strata accumulated. Thus, the face of France—its people as well as its institutions—changed considerably.

First, Christianity was established as the state-endorsed religion. By about 900, the Church had become a true political, economic, and cultural power. Immigrants less civilized by Western (Roman) standards were exposed through Christianity to ideas of law and government, to writing, and to Latin. Ironically, this civilizing process was a continuation of a pagan movement—Romanization—begun in the first century B.C. A second important change in France was the shift of the locus of power from the south to the north—the area least Romanized and most inhabited by immigrants at the dawn of the Middle Ages. After five hundred years of subservience to the south (Rome and the more developed southern provinces of Gaul), the north finally came into its own. The nucleus of the soon-to-be-established dynastic kingdom of France was centered on the Paris-Orléans axis, later known as the Île-de-France. The north experienced its first real prosperity through maritime trade at ports on the English Channel and the North Sea; and it provided its first native-son leaders, most of whom were Germanic in origin.

In the last half of the sixth century, Clovis was one such leader. The grandson of a ruler named Merovech—from whom comes the name of the Merovingian Dynasty—Clovis succeeded his father to the throne in 481 or 482. The king converted to Christianity in either 496 or 506. All French rulers would henceforth be Christian (though an echo of Clovis' gesture occurred about a thousand years later, when Henri of Navarre also felt it politically expedient to convert from Protestantism to Catholicism, the faith of most of his future subjects.) Clovis extended his rule over the various clans—the Franks and Alemanni—and thus brought under his leadership most of Gaul except for Burgundy and Provence.

Upon Clovis' death in 511, his realm was divided among his four sons. Though they fought bitterly, they nonetheless managed to extend their influence into Burgundy, Bavaria, and parts of Saxony. Family strife continued into the next generation, notably between Chilperic and his wife Fredegund in the northwest of Gaul and Sigebert and his wife Brunhilda in the northeast. Warfare was a fact of life; Bretons and Gascons in the west, Lombards in the southeast, and Avars in the east all exerted pressure on the Merovingian domain.

In 639 the realm was divided yet again upon the death of its ruler, Chilperic's grandson, Dagobert (immortalized in a children's song still sung today in France). The Merovingian dynasty was on the wane; the last kings were mere puppets. Most power in the various regional palaces was actually in the hands of officials known as "mayors."

One such "mayor" was Pepin III the Short, the son of a powerful mayor and the father of Charlemagne. Pepin deposed the last Merovingian king, Childeric III, in 750. One year later, after removing his own nephews from government, he had himself proclaimed king with the approval of the pope. Fifty years later, Charlemagne would be crowned emperor of all the Romans—a title whose precise significance is still a matter of much debate. Was this the pope's idea in order to bind Charlemagne, as king of the Franks, to the Roman cause? And who exactly were these Romans anyway? The inhabitants of Rome or those of all the papal states? Whatever the case may be, the title of Roman Emperor must have increased Charlemagne's prestige, especially in the non-Frankish realms over which he ruled.

Charlemagne

The political acts and personal attributes of this important figure shed light not only on the changing map of Europe, but also on certain early medieval values that may seem foreign today. We are fortunate to have a biography of Charlemagne, the *Vita Karoli Magni*, written by one of his learned courtiers, Einhard. The latter lived at the court beginning in 795, knew Charlemagne well, and considered him the embodiment of the ideal king, as did many of his contemporaries. Some modern historians share that view, citing as one proof of his greatness the cultural renaissance that occurred during his reign. By all accounts, medieval and modern, Charlemagne displayed characteristics that appear incompatible in twenty-first-century moral standards: he was fair-minded but also vengeful, faithful but lusty, cultured but rough, forever pious but often ruthless. Some historians contend that he did little more than realize the expansionist goals established by his father.

Indeed, Charlemagne must have shared his father's will to power. When still a boy, Charlemagne—then called only Charles— accompanied his father on military expeditions to reassert control over Aquitaine and thereby extend the kingdom all the way to the Pyrenees. Through such training, Charles learned how to fight against all odds to increase his territory, even if this required usurping the rights of relatives. Upon the death of Pepin in 768, in accordance with Frankish custom, the kingdom was divided between his two sons: Charles (the future Charlemagne) and the younger Carloman. Shortly thereafter, Charles conspired with the king of Lombardy (Italy) against Carloman. When Carloman died in 771, Charles ignored the succession rights of his brother's sons, who fled to the Lombard king for protection. Charles immediately and successfully waged war against his former ally (and current father-in-law), erasing the nephews from the historical record in the process. (We recall that Pepin had also disposed of his own potentially troublesome nephews.) Rumors abounded that Charles had ordered his relatives put to death, though this suspicion was never confirmed.

In the space of a decade, Charles managed to unite into one tremendous empire practically all the Christian lands of Western Europe except for southern Italy, the British Isle, and Asturias in Spain. Based on this feat alone, he earned the title Charles the Great (Carolus Magnus or in French, Charlemagne). During the rest of his reign, he was involved in defending his territory.

Like the depiction of him in the "Song of Roland," and like most medieval sovereigns, Charlemagne incarnated the law; he took it entirely upon himself to mete out justice and punishment. Though Charlemagne held the Church in high regard, he asserted his suzerainty over it, believing that he was answerable only to himself and to God. This gave him a free hand in dealing with all those he considered enemies of his empire or of the Church. For example, between 772 and 804, Charlemagne conducted numerous actions against the Saxons whose continued resistance he considered treacherous, since they had agreed some years previously to be incorporated into his empire and Christianity. Charlemagne's treatment of them became increasingly violent; in 782, he had an estimated 4,500 Saxons executed. Extreme measures such as these even drew the criticism of some within his immediate entourage—Alcuin, for example, his trusted adviser and head of his palace school. By 804 Charlemagne had achieved his goal of completely subduing the Saxons, though at a great cost of human life.

The French historical imagination juxtaposes this image of a ruthless despot with that of a benevolent ruler who encouraged a veritable cultural and educational renaissance in his kingdom. Neither image is false; both must be taken into account in order to begin to understand Charlemagne and the early Middle Ages. In order to re-establish centers of learning in France, Charlemagne brought scholars from all corners of his realm, like Einhard and Alcuin, and many from beyond its borders. He himself learned some Latin and Greek as an adult, and had many books read aloud to him. Moreover, education extended beyond the royal court. Throughout the Carolingian empire, young Frankish knights received instruction in the new academies; the clergy benefited from intensive study of Latin and theology in monastic and cathedral schools; and steps were taken toward providing education for children. Though this last goal would not reach fruition until the late nineteenth century, Charlemagne has retained his image as a father of primary education. (French textbooks for many decades included sketches of the medieval leader surrounded by young pupils.) The intellectual, cultural, and educational movements that Charlemagne inspired and supported are customarily referred to as the "Carolingian renaissance."

After the death of Charlemagne in 814, his legacy grew. He became an illustrious exemplar for later rulers of Europe, many of whom realized the importance of keeping the memory of this secular, saintly emperor alive in the minds of their subjects. In 1000 Otto III of Germany had Charlemagne's tomb opened; in

A familiar image of Charlemagne surrounded by schoolchildren. According to popular legend, he was keenly interested in primary education.

1165 Frederick Barbarossa had him canonized; and Philippe Auguste of France, who reigned from 1179 to 1223, boasted that he was a direct descendant of the great leader. (In fact, Philippe's ancestors had seized power from Charlemagne's true descendants.) Charlemagne became the object of a liturgical cult in churches in France, Germany, and even parts of Spain and Italy—areas that once comprised his great empire. Although his empire survived him by only one generation, the constitutional traditions he established prevailed in the kingdoms of France and Germany for centuries.

Life under the Feudal System (900–1300)

The solidarity of counts, bishops and abbots that had been so painstakingly established by Charlemagne proved impossible to maintain. The first Capetian kings of France—Hugh Capet (987–996) and Robert Capet (996–1031)—possessed hardly more power than ordinary overlords. The difficulty they had in extending their dominion much beyond the Ile-de-France reveals feudalism's functioning, and lack of functioning, during the tenth and early eleventh centuries.

"Feudalism" was (as it is today) a very broad term in the Middle Ages that encompassed a variety of relationships and obligations. In principle, the feudal system involved service owed by a vassal to his lord in exchange for land—a fief that remained under the ultimate control of the lord. Vassals were required to provide military service, pay dues, and accept their lord's judgments in legal disputes and in matters of marriage and succession. In practice, it did not always work that way. On occasion, a given lord and the men he considered his vassals might have quite different notions of the rules governing their relationship. The fluid understanding of feudal relations contributed to the volatile atmosphere that marks this time period. Prior to the reign of Louis VI (1108–1137), the crowned heads of France could not expect consistent and unconditional service from their lordly vassals.

Feudal lords acted in their own interests. If foreign invaders threatened their personal domains—as was the case in the eleventh century when Vikings and Saracens attacked—the lords would arm themselves and fight. But fighting for the "nation" was not yet part of the general consciousness. In many areas of France, threats came more from one's immediate region than from exotic pagan lands. There were often arms races, in which all the barons of a particular area felt compelled to compete against each other, to flaunt the superiority of their armies and fortified bastions, and to attempt to press their adversaries' knights into service.

This was the chaotic reality of feudalism that greeted Louis VI, referred to as Louis the Fat when he ascended the throne of France in 1108. In the course of his thirty-year reign, he managed to recover control over the unruly barons in the Île-de-France and the Orléans region. In so doing, he brought to the French crown its first real power and dignity, set the scene for further expansion, and re-established the Carolingian paradigm that the king is a vassal of no man.

Peasants: Slaves and Serfs

The eleventh and twelfth centuries experienced renewed economic prosperity, the main source of which was agriculture. Skirmishes among lords did not, of course, cease. If anything, a series of good harvests in the early part of the eleventh century gave these barons more to fight over. There was certainly an interest in acquiring more tillable land by whatever means necessary. Land that had lain fallow for centuries was put into cultivation; forests were cleared and, in some cases, land was reclaimed from the sea.

The pool of laborers on medieval fiefs included free peasants, serfs, and slaves who were hereditarily bound to their tenements. Certain conditions, like poor harvests or roving bands of marauders, could lead freemen to give up their liberty. At least as serfs or slaves these peasants felt themselves under the protection of a strong lord, though in fact they continued to be vulnerable. Peasants always ran the risk of being slaughtered—their huts and crops mercilessly burned—by troops under orders to financially ruin a lord.

Like most other aspects of feudalism, serfdom and slavery varied from region to region. For instance, on the borders of Saxony, slaves from pagan areas further to the east provided a cheap source of labor, enabling the indigenous peasants to retain their freedom. In all areas of France, slavery diminished as the Church took an increasingly dim view of enslaving people converted to Christianity and as slave-holders came to realize that serfs, who worked for themselves and fed themselves for portions of every year, were a cheaper source of labor than slaves. By the ninth century, slavery as we know it—in which the slave, his

50

body and his offspring are owned and can be sold by another—was on the wane, and by the eleventh century, the castes of slave and serf were largely indistinguishable.

Urban Development

From the eleventh through the thirteenth centuries, the political importance of towns and their citizens grew. The income of towns came from a number of sources: the manufacture of tools and clothing, local markets (involving market fees paid to the overlord of the town), and occasional trade with more distant places. A town possessing rare religious relics might also attract pilgrims, who would create more business for the town's merchants as well as make offerings to the local church.

Towns that had existed under the Romans were refurbished, and local nobles and dukes sponsored entirely new towns for defensive, economic, and colonization purposes. A baron who started a successful town could enjoy revenue from the rents, fair and market tolls, and trade tariffs. The Duke of Gascony, Edward I of England, was particularly active in planning and supporting a type of new town, called a "bastide," in both southwestern France and England. Bastides were laid out on a rectangular grid modeled on Roman town plans. One advantage of such a grid plan was that it facilitated tax collection; for this purpose, city blocks were numbered for the first time in history. Towns built as medieval bastides are found throughout southwest France, often retaining the word "bastide" in their name, and still containing picturesque market squares surrounded by arcaded walkways and shops. (It is said that such bastides provided the model for

A bastide town of the kind built, according to a grid derived from Roman town plans, in southwest France and England in the 13th and 14th centuries. Bastides contain central marketplaces surrounded by arcaded shops.

the English colonists who built New Haven, Connecticut.) The bastides also serve as a reminder that parts of France were controlled for long periods by England and share certain traits with that country.

Despite the vested interest that nobles had in building and maintaining thriving towns, the inhabitants occasionally rose up against the overlords and the clergy. There was an ongoing struggle for increased rights for town dwellers—a struggle that would reach a bloody and unfortunate climax in the fourteenth century. In the first years of the twelfth century, the people of the town of Laon murdered the local bishop when he refused to grant them certain rights of self-government. Urban political movements, however, were not the rule throughout France. Many towns never revolted in any way; in fact, many enjoyed special rights granted by their overlords in order to increase immigration, and thereby their own revenues.

The population of Paris, and its merchant class in particular, enjoyed significant prosperity throughout this period. Guilds acquired considerable rights. For instance, the river-merchants' guild was allowed by the king (Louis VII, son of Louis VI) to buy the main Parisian port on the Seine in 1141; and thirty years later, this guild was granted a charter confirming its "ancient right" to a monopoly of river trade. Near the end of the century, during his yearlong absence from France, the king (Philippe II, son of Louis VII) entrusted the government of Paris to a guild, rather than to the otherwise powerful Provost of Paris. By the dawn of the thirteenth century, the crown had made an unprecedented move in relinquishing one of its own precious rights to the townsmen of Paris: the right to collect duty on incoming goods.

Despite the growth and prosperity of Paris and of French towns in general, city life was far from comfortable, at least by our standards. Though France had moved beyond the somber ages, progress was still slow and uneven. Public sanitation had actually deteriorated since the time of the Romans. Early twelfth-century Paris has been described as a place where pedestrians "avoided milch goats and roving swine. The old Roman paving stones, worn and askew, made beds for mud and household bilge, for dust and refuse, and scavengers with great rakes and besoms were forever raising stench and shifting filth from hole to hole. Never were the proud affirmation of man's immortality and the moldy evidences of his transiency so closely juxtaposed" (Kelly, 16–17).

Transportation

The great advances in transportation the Romans had made were not carried into the early centuries of the Middle Ages. In fact, the existing roadways deteriorated to such an extent that in most parts of France travel by wagon became nearly impossible, and trade was consequently limited to goods that could be carried on a horse or donkey. By the end of the Middle Ages, this dismal situation had radically changed: France had planned and built a national system of roads on which various sorts of vehicles were able to move passengers and freight.

Several factors contributed to these changes. First, the advent of the Crusades made the need for roadways a pressing issue for the Catholic Church. Once underway, the nearly hundred-year long series of Crusades exposed French soldiers to the more

For many centuries, builders recycled materials from existing structures, yielding a mixture of styles from different eras.

advanced technology of the eastern lands; the Hungarians, for example, were highly competent in the design of wheeled vehicles. Besides encouraging Crusades to the Holy Land, the Church exhorted Christians to go on pilgrimages to European sites associated with the early martyrs and miracles. The Church consequently established religious orders whose mission was to improve roadways and bridges and provide aid to travelers. We might think of these medieval specialists as early civil engineers. Their activity improved roads to the point that carriages of all sorts could easily travel long distances; the implications for national and international trade, as well as for military deployment, are clear. It is worth noting, however, that military concerns were not the foremost factor in the improvement of medieval land transportation—as had been the case with the Romans—but rather the movement of people for religious purposes.

The Church: Monasticism

Along pilgrimage and trade routes, monasteries were often built to house and feed travelers. Monastic life played a valuable social role in providing a place for thousands to live and work, in particular the landless—a class that included many nobles who either had no land or were younger sons and could not inherit. Due to their numbers and the organization of their orders, monasteries became a powerful economic and cultural force.

Of course, the goal of medieval monasteries was not explicitly economic but rather spiritual. In striving to spread Christianity, monasticism can largely be credited with preserving literacy—and ancient manuscripts—during the early Middle Ages. On a political level, monasticism established, or at least reinforced, the authority of the pope over all secular leaders. In so doing, it eroded the notion of the king as the direct representative of God.

The most important monastic movements were undertaken by the Benedictine community at Cluny in the tenth century, and by the Cistercian order in the twelfth century. Each order was founded in a spirit of reform, though each eventually came to be criticized for some of the same flaws that it had criticized in its predecessors—chiefly, excessive involvement in worldly matters.

The order of Cluny, founded in 910 by Duke William the Pious of Aquitaine, preached a return to the strict observance of the Benedictine Rule. It developed a systematized centralization hitherto unknown in monastic orders, and considered the pope its sole authority. Members of the monastic order of Cluny were the first to state explicitly that war could benefit the souls of those who undertook it. From this ideal, the promulgation of crusades became a papal prerogative, and a king's role as a war leader was thus diminished. When there were nearly two thousand Cluniac monasteries in the twelfth century, the pope claimed that *all* wars fell within papal jurisdiction. In short, the authority of the pope continued to grow at the expense of the crown; for example, kings lost their control over episcopal appointments.

But by this time in the twelfth century, Cluny itself was being criticized for its wealth and the worldliness of its adherents. The accumulation of money and property was seen to involve monks in unseemly disputes. Cluny was indeed closely tied to the most powerful noble families in France: many of them placed their younger sons in Cluniac monasteries, and contributed great sums and real estate to the abbeys in their domains. Cluny was further criticized for instigating short novitiates for these noble children, and thus filling the clergy with men unsuitable for a spiritual life. Two other abuses of the churchmen were particularly under fire: married priests and simony (buying or selling church offices or benefices).

Some of the most vocal critics of corrupt monastic orders were themselves monks. The Cistercians—a Roman Catholic monastic order founded in 1098 in Cîteaux (Latin: Cistercium), a locality near Dijon—demanded severe asceticism and rejected all revenues from the landed gentry. Like the Cluniacs, the Cistercians' tight system of administration posed a special threat to secular power; monks were governed exclusively by their own leaders, not the king. The newer order, however, was even more bound to the decisions made by the abbots in charge.

An important difference between the Cluniacs and the Cistercians is that the latter required their monks to engage in manual labor. Though most of the farm-like, austere abbeys run by the Cistercians were located far from the beaten path, they underwent tremendous and rapid growth. This development was undoubtedly due to the fact that each abbey enjoyed such a disciplined, unpaid labor force, and that the Cistercians were able to farm without the hindrances of feudal customs. These monasteries developed new techniques of farming, and even of marketing, despite the official distaste of the order's founders for commerce.

The Cistercians thus played an undeniable role in the economic progress of the twelfth century. Even before the close of that century, however, some of the Cistercian abbeys were accumulating wealth by accepting churches, villeins, and tithes and by commercial transactions in wool and grain. This business was a violation of one of their most essential principles. They were

Medieval illustration of an abbey under construction.

The roof of Chartres (13th century).

*Notre Dame de Paris, the most famous of the Gothic
cathedrals (12*th*–13*th *centuries). It was constructed on the site
of a Gallo-Roman temple dedicated to Jupiter.*

condemned by many for their own lack of discipline, and their tight self-regulatory administration began to crumble. Rather than electing their own abbots, the pope started to appoint abbots who were sometimes not themselves Cistercians and whose sole role was to protect and increase revenues.

These abbots were often able to wield considerable influence as counselors to both popes and to kings. Two renowned examples are Bernard de Clairvaux and Abbot Suger of Saint-Denis, also well known for his role in the development of Gothic architecture. Suger had the distinction of having been the schoolmate and close friend of Louis Capet, who became King Louis VI in 1108. It was Suger's belief that the king's role should be enlarged—as opposed to the progressive reduction in power that had occurred earlier—and that in presenting the king as a vassal of Saint-Denis, French nobles would unite under him for a worthwhile cause. Louis did indeed march into battle carrying the banner of Saint-Denis, the Oriflamme, and—as the story is often told—his German adversaries, seeing the symbol, retreated without fighting. The size of Louis' forces—the largest army he had ever amassed—undoubtedly had something to do with the retreat as well! Louis VII later named Suger regent when he left for the Second Crusade in 1147, though some feared the abbot might not return the crown upon the king's return. Their concerns were not justified.

Twelfth-Century Royalty: the Life of Eleanor of Aquitaine (1122–1204)

The great rulers of the Capetian and Plantagenet houses marked the twelfth century through their leadership, fortitude, and, above all, their burning rivalry with each other. Eleanor of Aquitaine was wife to both a Capet (Louis VII of France) and a Plantagenet (Henry II of England). One cannot study her life without learning of the entire era's royal intrigues; they are truly worthy of Shakespeare! Eleanor was at the center of power in France and England for most of her 82 years, crossing from one continent (and husband) to another, crusading to the Holy Land (and nearly staying there), and acting as patron for two major literary movements. Through all these events, she also managed to give birth to ten children, nine of whom lived beyond infancy—a considerable feat in an era of extremely high infant mortality.

Many French historians tend to focus on Eleanor's fifteen-year reign as the Queen of France, emphasizing the negative influence that she supposedly exerted over the king rather than the political sagacity and indomitable spirit she displayed later in her life. Following the lead of the primary medieval historian for Louis's reign, the Abbot Suger, modern French historians depict Eleanor as "frivolous" and "sensual," qualities that were "little compatible with the asceticism of the king." Furthermore, for the past eight hundred years, she has been accused of "ridiculing" the King Louis VII of France, in particular when she accompanied him on the Crusade to the Holy Land. English historians of Eleanor are similarly myopic and limit their studies to Eleanor as Queen of England and the mother of two significant, if not consistently illustrious, English kings: Richard I the Lion-Heart and King John (surnamed Lackland until he outlived his brothers and thus inherited a vast domain).

A study of Eleanor's entire life, however, gives us a view of the spirit and contours of twelfth-century France, as well as of the extent to which national alliances and borders were vulnerable to change. "Nations" in the modern sense of the term were still in an embryonic state. The domain controlled by Eleanor's father, William X, Duke of Aquitaine, was larger than the domain held by the French king at that time. It is little wonder that Eleanor was a prime marriage prize! The fact that she intended to govern her own lands, even after her marriage to Louis VII, infuriated the king's counselors who had supposed that France would quickly annex the huge territory in Western France. This was not the last time that Eleanor's actions would surprise and dismay a royal court.

French historians are undoubtedly justified in pointing to the incompatibility between Eleanor and the French king, although it was perhaps less personal than cultural. At the time of their marriage in 1137, the court of Aquitaine could boast of a more highly cultured elite than the court in Paris. The arts had flourished under Eleanor's father, who was himself a poet of some renown. To a young woman reared in the warmth and culture of the southwest, the royal court in Paris must have seemed a dismal and cold place. She may have had to learn the language of the north, the *langue d'oi*, which was quite different from the *langue d'oc* spoken in various forms throughout the south of France.

The great urban renewal in Paris would be undertaken only in the last years of the twelfth century, under the reign of Philippe Auguste (Louis VII's son by a subsequent wife). The Paris to which Eleanor arrived as a bride bore no resemblance to what we see today, or even to what Paris became in the later Middle Ages. The royal quarter in early twelfth-century Paris has been described thus:

"[Here] the Capets still held their court in the ancient tower and precincts of the Merovingian kings. There rose the fortress pile that 'shouldered above the roofs of the whole city,' tunneled with dim passages and hollow stairs giving access to somber rooms and glowering chambers that seemed quarried from the solid stone" (Kelly, 15).

Eleanor's young husband Louis was as austere as the fortress that housed him. He had been reared in a monastery and was unprepared for his ascension to the throne in 1131. In an act that was viewed by many as impulsive and rash, Louis seized land belonging to one of his most powerful vassals, Thibaut, Count of Champagne. A civil war ensued in 1142. Peace was finally negotiated (by Abbot Suger), but prominent ecclesiastics condemned some of Louis' actions—especially the massacre of peasants in a church. Many in this group blamed Eleanor for having encouraged Louis to undertake the perilous venture. Most biographers of the couple contend that Louis displayed his love of Eleanor, even in public, in a way that was uncommon for the time period and for people of their rank. If this is true, Eleanor may indeed have exerted considerable influence over him in the early years of their marriage.

Following the war with Thibaut, Louis mended his relations with the Church, in part by leading a massive crusade to free the Holy Land as penance for his massacre of the innocent peasants in Champagne. On this crusade, Eleanor aroused Louis's jealousy when she threatened to remain with her uncle in Antioch. Upon returning to France, they were reconciled for a few years; but in 1152, Louis asked for and was granted an annulment by the pope. In fifteen years of marriage, the couple had produced only two daughters. Like the infamous Henry VIII of England four hundred years later, Louis was undoubtedly preoccupied with having a male heir and argued for the annulment of his marriage based on consanguinity, a common problem to this day among European royal houses. (Unlike Henry VIII, however, he did not resort to the chopping block to rid himself of an unwanted wife.) Although there were other reasons for Louis and Eleanor to end their marriage, the lack of sons was clearly a most pressing issue.

Within two years, Eleanor married the man who would soon become King of England, Henry II, to whom she bore five sons and three daughters. Since Eleanor maintained her lands as she departed the throne of France, Henry was able to unite a huge territory—the so-called Angevin Empire—consisting of Aquitaine, Anjou, Normandy, Maine, Touraine, and Brittany. Until the 1170s, Eleanor spent most of her time in her native Aquitaine, administering her own realm. It was during these years that she held a highly cultured and literary court at Poitiers that was frequented by the most famous poets (troubadours) of the day. She was patron to two poetic movements: the courtly love tradition and the historical legends of Brittany.

One can only wonder what would have emerged from Eleanor's court at Poitiers had it continued until the end of her long life. As well as being a cultural center, however, it was a political hotbed. Here her sons plotted against their father, probably entering into collusion with the King of France. Eleanor's precise role has never been determined; but she did offer her sons military support. When their revolt failed, she attempted to flee to France and the safety of her former husband's court. She never made it that far, however.

Captured en route, she was taken to England where she was imprisoned until the death of Henry in 1189.

Except for the repeated interludes when Henry's sons were in revolt, their territory on the continent posed a constant threat to the Capetians: first to Louis VII, and then to his son Philippe Auguste. There were long-standing disputes between the two powers over the regions of the Vexin (between Normandy and the Île-de-France), the Berry, and Auvergne. By 1188 Philippe was able to exploit the rift between Henry and his son, Richard the Lion-Heart. Philippe first gained the homage of Richard and then, the following year, forced Henry to renounce his claim to the Auvergne. Henry died two days later, at which time Richard ascended to the throne.

Again, a Plantagenet and a Capet formed an alliance—this time in order to go on yet another Crusade—and again the alliance soured. Philippe returned before Richard from the Holy Land, and immediately set about attacking the Plantagenet continental possessions. This was a breach of the vow asked of all crusaders: to protect the holdings of fellow crusaders in the homeland. Philippe's plans were furthered by the convenient capture of Richard by the Duke of Austria. Philippe did everything within his power to prolong Richard's captivity; but Richard was at last released in 1194, after the payment of a large ransom that Eleanor helped collect and personally delivered to her son's captor.

A fortuitous event changed the course of twelfth-century history: the untimely battlefield death of Richard the Lion Heart in 1199. He died with no heir. Fearing the demise of the Plantagenet line, eighty-year old Eleanor immediately traveled to Spain to get her granddaughter, Blanche of Castile, and marry her to Philippe's son. That same year, Eleanor helped to defend Aquitaine and to hold Mirabeau, thereby securing a large part of her son John's possessions on the continent.

But even with his mother's help, the youngest Plantagenet son was no military match for Philippe. While John was attempting to assume the crown (a contested ascension), Philippe was able to regain long-lost lands through negotiation and armed strength. Philippe conquered Normandy and subdued Maine, Touraine, Anjou, and most of Poitou. By 1213, less than a decade after Eleanor's death, her worst fears had been realized: the Anglo-Angevin power on the continent had been greatly undermined—indeed, it had been broken.

The Last of the Capetians (1179–1328)

Philippe Auguste reigned for forty-four years (1179–1223). As just discussed, he conquered the continental lands held by the Plantagenets and thus greatly expanded the borders of France—almost to the size it is today. But Philippe did much more. He continued the long process of bringing the French nobility under the control of the crown. He instituted a new appointed class of officers, who were to supervise on a local level, to mete out justice, to call up armed forces when necessary, and, importantly, to collect the revenues in the now vast domain. In the ongoing struggle between merchants and nobles, Philippe strengthened the former by helping them to free themselves from the burden of seignorial privileges. Existing towns flourished during his reign and many new towns were founded—all of which contributed to the wealth of the central royal power. Paris was rejuvenated: new thoroughfares were constructed within the city, and a new rampart around it. Under Philippe Auguste, Paris started to become the great city that it is today.

The true successor to Philippe Auguste was not his son but his grandson, Louis IX, who ruled from 1226–1270, and was highly loved and respected by his subjects. Louis IX instigated a great many administrative, judicial, and fiscal reforms; curbed warfare among barons; and strongly opposed the expansion of clerical powers. Although strongly authoritarian, he respected provincial custom and the local rights based upon it. Townspeople and peasants must have seen in their king an ally who would protect them from the costly skirmishes of the nobles and from fiscal mismanagement. For instance, between 1259 and 1262, he removed thirty-five communes from the control of urban governors who had unjustly overtaxed them. Henceforth, all fiscal administration of these communes was controlled directly by his court.

Later Capetian kings did not reign with quite the same piety and concern for the populace that Louis IX had displayed; though they did increase the territory controlled by the crown and the power of the crown itself. As usual, marriage was a prime source of land. Through marriages, the areas of Champagne, Navarre, and Burgundy were added to France. Other acquisitions were the result of purchases or treaties. For the most part, Capetian rulers maintained what had become traditional policies toward the nobility and towns; but this was not the case for relations with the church, especially during the reign of Louis IX's grandson, Philippe le Bel.

This Philippe, who ruled from 1285–1314, is a fascinating subject for the kind of psychological profile that, unfortunately, would go beyond the limits of this volume. Suffice it to say that he had a troubled childhood after losing his mother, Isabella of Aragon, at the age of three; and that, throughout his youth, it was rumored that his stepmother was trying to kill him and Isabella's other sons. Philippe is depicted as insecure and mistrustful. In his defense, however, it must be recognized that he called for investigations into the conduct of royal officials that led to beneficial fiscal reforms, much like those enacted by his illustrious grandfather. Unlike Louis IX, however, Philippe le Bel managed to offend and alienate nearly everyone: nobles, townsmen, and ecclesiastics.

In taxing the clergy without papal approval, Philippe brought down on himself the ire of Pope Boniface VIII, who suspended the crown's right to tax the Church in 1301 and called the French leaders of the Church to Rome to discuss the king's measures. In retaliation, Philippe had the papal bull publicly burned and vowed to see the pope judged for heresy and immoral deeds. A French minister was dispatched to Rome to seize Boniface; a skirmish ensued; the pope was liberated after two days of captivity, but died the following month. Philippe continued his vendetta against the pope posthumously, and saw to it that the next popes—Benedict XI and Clement V (who was of Gascon origin)—were more amenable to the interests of France. It was Clement who moved the Holy See to Avignon where it would stay for nearly seventy years, despite repeated efforts by the Church to return it to Rome.

The English translation of Philippe IV's byname, "the Fair," should not be understood as a commentary on the justice of his acts. (He was dubbed "the Fair," "le Bel," on the basis of his blond hair and complexion.) We can only condemn some of his actions. In 1306 he expelled all Jews from France, seizing their property for the crown. This expulsion was the climax of years of anti-Semitism that had been condoned by the canonized Louis IX, as by other Capetian kings before him. The year following the Jewish expulsion, Philippe turned his attention to the Knights Templar—an independent order founded in the twelfth century to financially support the Crusades. Members of the order were seized and tortured to exact "confessions" from them to be used in Philippe's case against them before the pope. Though the crown gained financially from the demise of the Knights Templar, some historians are still puzzled by the vehemence of Philippe's attack of them. It is possible that the king, who seemed to model himself after his saintly grandfather, felt that he too was called by God to prosecute (and persecute) all people he considered sinners or heretics.

This intolerance also marked the short reigns of Philippe IV's three sons, the last of whom, Charles IV, is particularly known for his failures—for instance, his unsuccessful invasion of Aquitaine and Flanders, and his bid for the German throne. With Charles' death in 1328, the direct line of Capetian kings begun in 987 came to an end. For all the failings of some of these rulers, they must nonetheless be credited with laying the foundation of the French nation-state.

CHAPTER THREE

FROM WAR TO REBIRTH: THE FOURTEENTH, FIFTEENTH, AND SIXTEENTH CENTURIES

Hard Times: The Fourteenth Century

Most historical descriptions of the fourteenth century paint a bleak picture of the times. In her study of the century, *A Distant Mirror: the Calamitous 14th Century*, Barbara Tuchman concludes: "It was a time of default. Rules crumbled, institutions failed in their functions. Knighthood did not protect; the Church, more worldly than spiritual, did not guide the way to God; the towns, once agents of progress and the commonweal, were absorbed in mutual hostilities and divided by class war; the population, depleted by the Black Death, did not recover. The war of England and France and the brigandage it spawned revealed the emptiness of chivalry's military pretensions and the falsity of its moral ones. The schism shook the foundations of the central institution, spreading a deep and pervasive uneasiness. People felt subject to events beyond their control, swept, like flotsam at sea, hither and yon in a universe without reason or purpose. They lived through a period that suffered and struggled without visible advance. They longed for a remedy, for a revival of faith, for stability and order that never came" (580).

The century did indeed begin badly. The climate across Europe was changing; in two successive winters (1306 and 1307), the Baltic Sea completely froze over, followed in the next decade by devastating floods. Famine was widespread as crops either froze or were inundated. The anxiety caused in our own time by global warming and recurrent natural disasters can perhaps help us understand the feelings of powerlessness of fourteenth-century Europeans when faced with such calamities.

We must keep in mind, however, that the medieval world is, to borrow Ms. Tuchman's metaphor, *a distant mirror* in which our faces are only faintly reflected. The inhabitants of the medieval world are far from us in both time and mentality; many of them perceived the climatic changes and resulting famines as ominous signs of God's wrath or of the impending Apocalypse. By engaging in acts of self-flagellation or by persecuting Jews, many medieval people thought they could mollify God and thereby end His successive scourges.

Into this already troubled scene the Black Death galloped, killing more people than any other known epidemic or war up to that time. The plague swept through Europe in repeated outbreaks between 1347 and 1351. The French chronicler Jean Froissart wrote that about one-third of Europe's population died, and modern historians are inclined to confirm his dire estimate, placing the death toll at around 25 million. Some cities, like Toulouse, lost up to half of their populations; some towns ceased to exist altogether.

The economic consequences in France were catastrophic: a severe labor shortage, countless uncultivated fields, and famine for the second time in the century. There were psychological consequences as well, some of which can be detected in the poetry, sculpture, and painting of the time. Europe was understandably preoccupied with death.

As if cold, famine, and plague were not enough, France was also racked by wars throughout most of the fourteenth century. A problem of succession was the ostensible first cause, though, as the decades wore on and the fighting continued, the war's purpose became increasingly unclear. When Charles IV died in 1328, Edward III of England considered himself a legitimate claimant to the crown. He was Charles' first cousin and already in possession of a large portion of southwestern France (Guyenne). However, a French assembly, wary of conferring the crown on an English king, chose instead a contender from the Valois royal line—Philippe VI. What is referred to as the Hundred Years War began when Philippe VI attempted to confiscate Guyenne. There followed a series of sieges, treaties, and breaches of treaties that kept France involved in costly conflict at precisely the time when its energies could have been directed at easing human suffering and building (and rebuilding) the economic structure of the beleaguered country.

Wars are sometimes credited with sparking economic growth, but this was certainly not the case in the Hundred Years War. French laborers and farmers—in fact most French not of noble blood—paid a heavy toll in the form of special taxes to fund the war effort, as well as of goods eaten, stolen, and ruined by the soldiers. Armies made no provisions to feed their vast numbers or, often, to pay them. Soldiers were simply expected to live off the land and whatever spoils they could appropriate. Understandably, the general public showed no enthusiasm for wars from which they stood only to lose materially.

Whereas troubadours had formerly extolled the virtues of the ideal knight in their epics, fourteenth-century moralists wrote treatises lambasting contemporary soldiers for the empty chivalric pomp that they displayed in tournaments and for the frequency of their defeats on the battlefield—the latter seen to be a direct result of the frivolous life they led. A university chancellor in Paris, Jean Gerson, drew an unflattering comparison between the knights of his own time and ancient Roman troops who, he contended, "did not drag after them three or four pack horses and wagons laden with robes, jewels, carpets, boots, hose, and double tents. They did not carry with them iron or brass stoves to make little pies" [Tuchman, 439].

At the close of the century, the condemnation of knights' behavior on military expeditions was voiced in even stronger terms. The Monk of St. Denis, for example, goes on at length about the debauchery of knights. He reserves particular outrage for those who participated in the Battle of Nicopolis in 1396—the last great battle and defeat of the century—where the Turks soundly crushed the European crusaders. According to medieval accounts, fine wines and foods were transported by boat to feed the officers, who dined with prostitutes they had brought along on the campaign. The lower ranking conscripts were given free license to do as they pleased with the women they found in villages along their route. Churchmen who had accompanied the troops on what was intended as a religious crusade apparently pleaded for moderation, but to no avail.

Medieval moralists, most of whom wrote of Nicopolis well *after* the battle, were quick to attribute the stunning defeat of the crusaders to their debauchery. What must also be considered in this battle, as in the frequent skirmishes comprising the Hundred Years War, is the fact that the French had not altered their military strategy for generations. One could argue, in fact, that they had no real strategy at all; rank, privilege, and the ephemeral quest for glory took precedence over tactical advantages. Whereas the British had realized that placing archers in the front lines of battle with the mounted cavalry behind them was tactically sound, the French continued to allow their mounted knights to ride first into battle. This unsound approach persisted because the noble knights would not tolerate having commoners precede them. Based on a profound disdain for the lower classes, this intransigence on the part of French nobility had dire consequences, as archers were thus forced to shoot *through* the mounted knights. This is but one example of an unwillingness to adapt practice to the exigencies of the actual battlefield. (A similar intransigence characterized the French military at the outset of World War II when generals were reluctant to place armored tanks in the avant-garde.) At Nicopolis, the situation was exacerbated by questions of pride and dissension among the European factions. In the decisive moment, a disastrous battle plan was imposed, many support troops fled the battlefield, and the rest were slaughtered by the Turks.

The lack of moral discipline among French knights had a corollary in the Catholic Church of the Avignon papacy (1309–77), which was accused of vices of all kinds: worldliness, debauchery, and simony. (For example, a would-be penitent could calculate

The infamous "rack," used from the mid-14th century to the end of the 18th century, that stretched the limbs of the suspect. Torture was a part of the legal process in most European countries, and was approved by the Catholic Church to root out heresy.

A catapult for propelling stones, spears, or other objects.
Variations on this mechanism were used in ancient times and
through the Middle Ages.

the cost of a pilgrimage to Jerusalem and then buy a pardon for that sum.) Petrarch, who had lived in Avignon, called it the "Babylon of the West." But criticism was not limited to the papacy; clerics at all levels were condemned in public opinion and mocked in literature. The popular French tales called *fabliaux*, for example, depict most friars as lechers or gluttons (or both).

The situation did not improve after the return of the papacy to Rome. From 1378 to 1417, there were still two—and at one point, three—rival popes, each one with different supporters, different sets of cardinals, and different administrators. The Schism, as it is now called, had a very negative effect on the Church and on European politics in general. It fed the fires of conflict between national groups and left the common people without spiritual exemplars.

New Perceptions: The Fifteenth Century

In spite of the hard times, or perhaps because of them, at the outset of the fifteenth century changes were occurring in the way individuals saw their world and their place within it. A sense of personal autonomy was emerging. Signs of such a shift had been evident even earlier in the Middle Ages. The sculptures adorning the portals of cathedrals bore increasingly individualized expressions (12th–13th century); painted and sculpted portraiture became more common (13th and 14th centuries); and biographies started to appear (as early as the 12th century). The composition of the family began to evolve as well. Knights started to live with their families in separate dwellings, rather than in the home of

*Sculpted relief of deathbed scene, abbey church in Moissac.
Deathbed scenes in sculpture, painting, and stained glass were
common from the 13th through the 16th century.*

Saint John the Baptist on the north portal at Chartres Cathedral, an early (13th century) example of the increased sense of individualism in the depiction of human figures.

their lord; and the younger sons of wealthy families were able to start their own households more frequently than in the heyday of feudalism, when they were expected to remain without landed inheritance. While it is true that these changes gave an elevated importance to the nuclear family in the thirteenth and fourteenth centuries, the individuals in those families remained bound to live according to societal rules that would seem to us quite rigid.

We can perhaps perceive more clearly the emergence of a personal sense of autonomy in the spiritual realm: the notion that salvation might be the result of a kind of inner self-transformation, rather than simply acquired by observing the required religious rites. The recurrent disasters of the fourteenth century undoubtedly made people at all social levels more open to claims made by mystics and small sects, most only marginally linked to the Church. In the course of the fifteenth century, individuals and sects that claimed to follow the commands of God *directly* came to be viewed by the Church as threat to ecclesiastical authority.

Joan of Arc: Personal Piety

Joan of Arc, perhaps the most celebrated heroine in French history, provides us with a poignant example of the trend toward reliance on individual spirituality as a guide to action. Born at the dawn of the fifteenth century, Joan refused to accept her allotted place in a fixed social caste, the peasantry, and acted under what she believed was divine guidance—a guidance that made her different from others (but not, it must be noted, from other female visionaries of the time).

At the age of sixteen, she asked for permission to join the forces of the Dauphin Charles, the son of the Valois king who was constantly contending with both the English and the Burgundians for control of the area where Joan lived, along the borders of the duchies of Bar and Lorraine in northeastern France. The fact that the king let a young girl engage in such a mission and provided her with troops gives testimony to the widespread belief in mystical visions (and, in Joan's case, mystical *voices*, since she claimed to receive her guidance orally from St. Michael, St. Catherine, and St. Margaret). Joan's presence must indeed have inspired the French soldiers, for they enjoyed a number of notable successes in their efforts to drive the Anglo-Burgundian forces from the land, some of them against serious odds. She created the conditions that made possible her pledged aim: the coronation of Charles in July 1429 at Rheims, a city formerly under English control.

Many details of Joan's activities, and even the nature of her mission itself, are unknown, disputed, or debated by historians and theologians. Through the centuries, the history of Joan of Arc has been colored by the prevailing ideologies and politics. What is known without doubt is that this young woman was trusted by King Charles and acted on his behalf—both as a soldier and a kind of unofficial counselor. We know that Joan was literate and wrote numerous letters to persuade opponents and functionaries to follow the king's (and her) will. Unfortunately, at the time of her trial and execution in 1431, there is no indication that her beloved king did anything to save her from the flames. She was condemned first by theological authorities, which then handed her case over to the secular officials. They summarily sentenced her to death. It is likely that what the Church considered most blasphemous in Joan's behavior and pronouncements was her claim to the authority of divine revelation, which made her answerable not to the Church, but only to God and the saints whose voices she followed. One hundred years later, the terrible religious wars across England and Europe turned on this same issue: the authority of the Church over the individual in matters of faith and fidelity.

Joan of Arc appears to rest secure in her sainthood, conferred in 1920, and in her role as a catalyst for French national consciousness. There is a certain irony in this latter role, for Joan of Arc was tried by a group of men almost exclusively French in origin. Furthermore, they were aligned at the time with the equally French Burgundians, who were themselves aligned with the English in their opposition to Charles as King of France. Joan of Arc did not accomplish her military goal of driving the English and their French allies out of northeast France; that would have to wait for two more decades, until the end of the Hundred Years War around 1453.

Humanism: Secular Piety

The term "humanism" was first used by nineteenth-century scholars to designate a European intellectual movement that emphasized the study of classical authors—Plato, Cicero, and Livy for example—and the development of human virtues: understanding, compassion, judgment, eloquence, and honor. In the fifteenth century, the European intellectual establishment underwent something akin to an invigorating blood transfusion when

Joan of Arc by Eugène Pascau. Painted shortly after her canonization in 1920.

"new" material from classical antiquity was rediscovered. Some of these texts had languished for many years in the libraries of monasteries under the control of scholar-clerics; others had arrived from the East, especially after the fall of Constantinople in 1453, when Eastern scholars fled to the West with their books and their scholarly traditions. The discovery of new modes of thought and inquiry served to loosen the mental strictures that had been imposed by the observance of strict religious dogma. Humanism inspired the individual to recognize his potential and become actively involved in contemplative as well as in civic matters.

In one sense, fifteenth-century humanists might have approved of Joan of Arc's heroic actions insofar as they were intended for the public good and involved a self-transformation of the individual. There is, however, one significant difference between a humanist and a mystic like Joan of Arc: the humanist's actions were based on *reason*, rather than on Christian faith alone. This distinction is not to imply that early humanists were atheistic or opposed to organized religion. Quite the contrary, many humanists were profoundly linked to the Church, and much humanistic activity in the fifteenth and sixteenth centuries was quite Christian in intent. Nonetheless, the classical emphasis of humanism— its reliance on texts from pagan Antiquity—was increasingly viewed by ecclesiastics as a challenge to Catholic orthodoxy. Even more threatening to the Church was research conducted by Humanists into Scripture itself. For instance, the Byzantine humanist and theologian Basil Bessarion (1403–1472) discovered that the supposed Dionysius the Areopagite drew his material from Plato. Although Bessarion was later made a Roman cardinal, not all Humanists were brought into the Catholic fold.

Over time, humanism was progressively associated with those who sought to reform the Catholic Church and whose efforts culminated in the Protestant Reformation and the Wars of Religion in the next century. Indeed, some of the religious reformers' goals resembled in spirit those of more secularly minded humanists—for instance, the desire that the individual come into direct contact with textual sources, whether from Antiquity or the Bible itself. Both movements emphasized the actions and duties of the individual, and both were dedicated to educating people at all social levels in order that they might better perform their civic and spiritual duties.

Tolerance and Cruelty: The Schizophrenic Sixteenth Century

Fifteenth-century Humanism was the first manifestation of a pan-European movement generally referred to as the "Renaissance," or "rebirth," which transformed the continent politically, socially, and aesthetically. Renaissance art forms and modes of thought migrated (much as the Black Plague had!) from south to north across Europe: beginning in Italy in the fifteenth century, moving into France in the sixteenth, and to England in the seventeenth. To name but three of the striking developments during the early phase of the Renaissance: Europeans began to explore the world on a grand scale, to accept the Ptolemaic view of the universe, and to print books that were able to reach a much wider public than manuscripts. It is no wonder that some historians and art historians of the eighteenth and nineteenth centuries, such as

Michelet in France and Burckhardt in Germany, saw it as shining proof of the inevitable march of progress.

Developments in art mirrored changes in attitude associated with humanism. Artists began to be considered true creators rather than mere artisans and technicians. The central focus of the plastic arts was placed on the dignity of the human being. In religious paintings, artists highlighted emotional drama; in portraits—like those of the French painter, François Clouet—the sitter is not depicted as a simple "type," but rather as a completely unique individual. Even in scientific works, such as Leonardo da Vinci's anatomical research, the human form was used as the standard for all proportions. Other art forms throughout Europe were similarly transformed. In France, the Pléiade group of poets broke with the complicated and rather mechanical versifying of their predecessors and proclaimed new poetic principles and sensibilities. The architecture of Pierre Lescot incorporated classical motifs and a respect for Renaissance proportions; the massive fortresses of the late Middle Ages were no longer built.

If one did nothing but study Renaissance art across Europe, it would be easy to draw the conclusion that this was indeed a time of beauty and harmony—a time in which the dignity of man was celebrated. Obviously, however, not every individual living in Renaissance Europe felt the positive effects of the new enlightened attitudes. For the most part, a person's identity continued to be grounded in his class, family, and community, although on each of these levels changes were occurring. The peasantry was particularly entrenched in age-old traditions and modes of behavior; peasants in France continued—even into the nineteenth century in some areas—to live in relative poverty and subjugation to forces beyond their control (wealthy landowners, nature, and the economic market). For every example of openness toward others in the Renaissance, one can cite a counter example of intolerance: the fascination with cultural differences discovered in the New World, for instance, coexisted with overt discrimination against Protestants and Jews in France.

French Renaissance Kings

When twenty-year old François I was crowned king in 1515, it must have seemed like a breath of fresh air to the French. He was quick-witted, handsome, and outgoing—quite a contrast to the long line of sickly and dour rulers who had preceded him. François began his reign in a spirit of optimism and tolerance. He greatly admired the Humanist Erasmus, and was a very active patron of the arts. He brought many artists (including Leonardo da Vinci) to France from Italy, then considered at the avant-garde of taste and refinement. François was also militarily successful, at least at first, when he conquered the long sought after Duchy of Milan. From that time on, François I was referred to as the knight-king and was immensely popular. He toured France tirelessly, visiting his subjects in remote areas, granting pardons to prisoners, and overseeing local judicial systems.

Unfortunately, François was soon mired in a vicious rivalry with King of Spain and Holy Roman Emperor, Charles V. François' problems began in 1525, when he was taken prisoner at the Battle of Pavia. Emperor Charles subsequently demanded over one-third of all the territory held by France as the price for his freedom. François refused categorically and remained in prison, where he wrote poetry and countless letters to his family and people. The French remained supportive of their king, even when he abdicated in favor of his son and signed a harsh treaty with Charles.

Despite the treaty, the surrendered French provinces refused to separate themselves from France—a stance that certain regions in France had taken in the early Middle Ages when England and France were trying to volley them from one sovereign to another. In both cases, the region's allegiance to a ruler was a matter of tradition, culture, and, of course, the region's attachment to a particular king. Such allegiance was sometimes hard to alter by the stroke of a pen.

The French might have had cause to become exasperated with the rivalry, however, for it appears that it was of a very personal nature, and the country at large did not stand to gain by it. The rivalry plagued France and its king for twenty-seven of his thirty-two years on the throne. Only the intercession of François' mother, whom he revered and whose advice he generally followed, prevented him from engaging in a personal duel with Charles. His mother later beseeched Charles' aunt, Margaret of Austria, to stop the destructive struggle between the two men. A treaty was signed that mitigated the earlier and harsher treaty, though the animosity between the kings remained a problem until their deaths.

The most pressing domestic problem for François was the religious ferment that was gaining momentum in the third decade of the century. Predisposed to religious tolerance, François was nonetheless shocked when reformers nailed a sign of protest to his bedroom door in 1534. Many cite this "Affair of the Placards" as a turning point in the attitude of the king toward the Protestants (usually referred to as Huguenots). When persecution increased, many Huguenots felt compelled to leave the country. The most famous of the exiles was Jean Calvin, whose *Institutes of the Christian Religion* was prefaced by a letter to François I that pleaded for tolerance. Despite the discrimination they suffered, the Huguenots increased their numbers in the following decades and became a national force that Catholics perceived as a threat.

François' son and the next king of France, Henri II, was more rigorous than his father in putting down the Huguenots. Shortly after Henri came to power in 1547, he created a special court for trying heretics; and in 1559, the last year of his reign, he laid the legal ground for subsequent persecution (the Edict of Écouen). Though Henri II accomplished some needed administrative reforms, his reputation among his countrymen never equaled that of his brilliant father. One of the more remarkable aspects of Henri II's reign was its end: he was hit in the eye by a lance while jousting in a tournament, and died ten days later. This event signaled the end of the medieval sport of jousting, and, in a sense, of knighthood in France. Feudalism, with its knights in shining armor, had by this time become anachronistic.

Three of Henri II's four sons by Catherine de Médici became the next kings of France—François II (1559–1560); Charles IX (1560–1574); and Henri III (1574–1589)—and his son-in-law was the celebrated Henri IV (1589–1610). François II was married to Marie de Guise, a member of a powerful French Catholic family (and the future Mary, Queen of Scots). François, who died after only a year in power, seemed to be a mere puppet of the Guises. His younger brother, Charles IX, was apparently intelligent but emotionally disturbed and very influenced by his mother, who acted as regent for him until 1563.

The events and intrigues leading up to the terrible massacre of Huguenots on St. Bartholomew's Day in 1572 involve, once again, rivalries within the royal court. It seems that Admiral Gaspard II de Coligny was at the point of convincing Charles IX to engage in war in the Low Countries against Spain. Catherine de Médici was against the plan, and perhaps jealous of the influence that Coligny exerted over her son. For these reasons—and others that we may never know—she consented to a botched assassination plot against Coligny. To cover up her part in the conspiracy, Catherine met with a group of Catholic nobles to plan the massacre of a great number of Huguenot leaders.

These leaders were in Paris to celebrate the wedding of Catherine's daughter, Margaret of Valois, to the Huguenot Henri of Navarre. The marriage was an effort to strengthen the peace that had been negotiated two years earlier between the two religious factions. Hopes ran high that this marriage would usher in a new era of mutual respect and cooperation. Alas, this was not to be.

On the night of August 23, 1572, soldiers of the Parisian forces were called to the Louvre—then the royal palace—and given orders to kill the Huguenots. The homes and businesses of Huguenots were burned and pillaged, and countless bodies were thrown into the Seine. The bloodshed spread to Rouen, Lyons, Bourges, Orléans, and Bordeaux. The death toll across France will never be known, though estimates run as high as

A contemporary depiction of the St. Bartholomew's Day Massacre, when thousands of Huguenots were slain throughout France.

70,000 dead. Archival records in Paris show that at least 3,000 Huguenots were slaughtered in that city alone.

The massacres exacerbated religious conflicts throughout Europe. Protestant nations—England and the Low Countries—were horrified, while Catholic countries such as Spain appeared to be relieved. The pope, Gregory XIII, went so far as to have a medal made to celebrate the event. Many Huguenots abandoned the Calvinist principles of obedience to royal authorities, formed a political party in 1573, and took up arms.

The next king of France, Henri III, had been present at the fateful meeting when prominent Catholics decided upon the massacre. Oddly enough, however, he did not find favor with these same Catholics once he ascended the throne two years later. Rather than relying on the crown to protect their interests, these leaders formed a powerful group, the Holy League. They were especially alarmed when a Huguenot, Henri of Navarre, became heir to the throne. Paris, a League stronghold, demonstrated against the succession, and Henri III was forced to leave the city. He ordered the assassination of the powerful Duke de Guise and his brother; and later, Henri III felt compelled to align himself with Henri of Navarre, his brother-in-law, former adversary, and former prisoner. Together the two Henris laid siege to Paris. During the fighting, a monk was allowed an audience with Henri III and promptly stabbed him. On his deathbed, the king named Henri of Navarre as his successor.

Much has been written about the figure of Henri of Navarre, known as Henri IV or Henri le Grand (reigned 1589–1610). He managed to bring peace and new prosperity to France, though most of his life was spent in combat. When he was not quite fourteen, he took part in a successful expedition against rebellious Roman Catholic nobles in Navarre; and a few years later, he distinguished himself in the Huguenot cavalry. His biographers imply that these early experiences, rather than whetting in the boy a desire to engage in knightly deeds, served to make him reflect on the disastrous effects of war on the population.

After being crowned King of France, Henri IV had to fight the Holy League for nearly a decade before his kingdom was secured. Many Catholic nobles and cities, Paris first among them, refused to give him their support. After much reflection, Henri decided to convert to Catholicism in order to end the religious strife in the land. The League could no longer oppose him once he was a Roman Catholic, though many doubted his sincerity, given his Huguenot background and past leadership of Huguenot armies. Nonetheless, French towns that had hitherto been staunchly opposed to him gradually began to pledge their

*Henri IV's birthplace in Pau. It is now a national museum with a
fine collection of Medieval and Renaissance tapestries.*

allegiance to the crown. It is likely that all but the most fanatic zealots were relieved to see the end of the long Wars of Religion. In March of 1594, Paris finally opened its gates to him, leading to one of the most oft-cited declarations in French history: "Paris is well worth a mass!"

An equally famous quotation attributed to Henri IV—"a chicken in every pot" ("une poule au pot")—gives us an idea of the nature of some of his achievements. Perhaps more than any French king before him, Henri IV acted to improve the lot of the lower classes in France. This he did without alienating the upper classes; in fact, he encouraged them to move forward economically after the long years of war and stagnation. The national debt plummeted, and he promoted development projects in agriculture and industry (for example silk production). As commerce prospered, new trade routes were built across France and new trade treaties were signed with other countries.

If Henri IV is one of the most popular characters in French history, it is not only because of his official record of achievements on the national scene. He is also known for his myriad love affairs, earning for him the title of "le vert galant," or "the old charmer." His marriage to Margaret de Valois was annulled by the pope in 1600, which allowed him to marry the princess of Tuscany, Marie de Médici—a union that produced five children, among them the future King Louis XIII. Henri IV was the first of the Bourbon kings of France, and, through his father, he was in the sole legitimate line of descent from the Capetian kings.

Henri IV was known for his flexibility when peace depended on it: he converted to Catholicism to save France from interminable religious strife, and opposed fanaticism of any kind. In

1598 he signed the Edict of Nantes, which established Catholicism as the official church of France, while according religious freedom to the Huguenots. Henri IV was assassinated in 1610 by a religious zealot—the very kind of person that the Edict of Nantes was intended to calm.

"Of Moderation": Michel de Montaigne (1534–1592) as a Case Study

Michel de Montaigne, born into the optimism of the early French Renaissance, was reared in the spirit of that time. His father had him taught Latin, the international language of culture and refinement, before he learned either French or Gascon—the local dialect in the southwest of France where the family estate was located. A Humanist sense of civic duty was also instilled in the young Michel, though he came into adulthood during the tumultuous Wars of Religion (1562–1598), during which Humanist ideals and political moderation were hard to maintain. Despite, or perhaps because of the difficulties of the times, Montaigne did his civic duty—agreeing to be mayor of Bordeaux (1581–1585), and serving as an occasional diplomat and negotiator for both Henri III and Henri IV. Montaigne remained a Catholic his entire life, though some members of his immediate family were Huguenot. Ironically, he was at times criticized by both religious factions; he nonetheless managed to maintain a delicate balance between the Catholic majority in Bordeaux and the Protestants.

It is not, however, for having fulfilled these public roles or for having maintained a moderate stance that Montaigne has gone

Michel de Montaigne (1533–1592).

down in history. He is most well known as the author of essays—a literary genre he virtually invented (and which Francis Bacon quickly adopted in English). Each essay, as its name implies, is a tentative exploration and questioning of a given subject or subjects, though the main subject of certain essays is not always apparent. The author digresses, and then advances by "fits and starts," giving an aura of immediacy, rather like the rambling development of thought itself. Judging by the titles of the hundred and seven essays, their ostensible subjects are far ranging: "Of Idleness," "That the taste of good and evil depends in large part on the opinion we have of them," "That to philosophize is to learn to die," "Of Moderation," "Of Friendship," "Of Smells," "Of the inconsistency of our actions," "Of Virtue," "Of the resemblance of children to fathers," "Of Cripples," and "Of Experience."

Underlying what appears to be a multifaceted project, however, is a nearly constant preoccupation with the "self." The reader learns at the outset of the *Essays* that the author takes himself as the "matter" of his texts. In Montaigne, the "self" is more central than even in the most human-centered Humanists of the fifteenth century. On this basis, one could argue that Montaigne's writing is a precursor to modern autobiography; but it is important to keep in mind that the *Essays* do not give voice—or only on rare occasions—to the author's emotional feelings or psychological reactions. The reader is nonetheless made aware of the visceral reactions of the author to the violence and intolerance of his world, and the sense of disappointment as he sees the intellectual optimism of the early Renaissance crumbling.

A prime example of Montaigne's reaction to cruelty is expressed, though obliquely, in the often-anthologized essay

"On Cannibals." This essay describes the customs of tribes indigenous to South America, about which the author had learned through the travel logs of European explorers. Rather than condemn the cannibalistic practices of these tribes, Montaigne emphasizes the profoundly civilized aspects of their culture, and criticizes Europeans for their practice of torturing people while still alive, as opposed to simply eating them once dead! For this tendency—rare in the sixteenth century—to criticize the failings of his own society while lauding the strengths of another, Montaigne has often been considered an early cultural relativist.

The *Essays* do not, however, preach cultural relativism, nor do they provide facile answers to the world's dilemmas. If Montaigne preaches anything, it is the importance of personal judgment, by which he means a kind of understanding arrived at through reflection and experience. He rejects the blanket acceptance of commonplaces and public opinion of the sort fostered in schools of his time. Rather than memorizing fixed abstract concepts, says Montaigne in his essay on education, students should learn through concrete experience.

In order to form such personal judgments, the "self" must be independent and free of the constraints of *a priori* notions. For Montaigne, the self is a site that, though ever changing and fragmented, is nonetheless more stable and certain than externally imposed claims to absolute knowledge. The skeptical query Montaigne took as his motto—"Que sais-je?" ("What do I know?")—is less an expression of complete negativity (in which case, the individual might renounce all attempts, or "essays," to form a judgment) than a challenge to the individual to look within, in order to accept his own limits and strengths without delusion.

In the following century, some religious leaders and thinkers attached Montaigne's skepticism as anti-Christian and self-absorbed. Other members of the educated elite in the seventeenth century, however, saw ideals in the *Essays* that they could endorse—in particular, the image of the wise, non-pedantic, and well-mannered gentleman. The great French philosopher René Descartes owes Montaigne a great deal. The essayist's rejection of appearances and his reliance on the "self" are not far from Descartes' prelude to his famous maxim: "I think, therefore I am." Subsequent generations—from eighteenth-century advocates of the Enlightenment to twentieth-century Post-Structuralists—have found in the *Essays* inspiration for their particular quests.

CHAPTER FOUR

CLASSICISM AND ENLIGHTENMENT: THE SEVENTEENTH AND EIGHTEENTH CENTURIES

Overview: the Triumph and Defeat of Absolutism

In a relatively short period of time—from the mid-seventeenth century until 1792—the French witnessed the elevation of the king into a kind of divinity and then, in a gesture unprecedented in their history, saw a king's head sliced off by the infamous Revolutionary guillotine. How did this amazing transformation in mentality occur in so short a time? Can we locate the cause in the so-called despotism of French kings of this time, or in the extreme poverty of large sections of the French population? As important as these factors were in contributing to the French Revolution, both must be seen in their historical context.

First, none of the French kings of this time was a despot in the modern sense of the word. Royal power in the seventeenth and eighteenth centuries was considered absolute because kings were thought to hold their power directly from God and thus rule in accordance with divine justice. Governance by divine right was not invented in this era; kings like Charlemagne and Saint Louis had been viewed as God's representatives on earth. But in the seventeenth century, the notion of divine right was emphasized in what we are tempted to call a public relations campaign. The effort was clearly intended to foster acquiescence to the king's absolute power by all his subjects. But absolutism does not imply that the king's every word was obeyed as law throughout the land—far from it.

The king had no national police force with which to impose his will. Nor was France a unified whole; it was still a somewhat federalist collection of provinces, each with its own legal customs and some with their own legislatures. Within each province there were social classes, estates, and professional groups that held their own rights and privileges. The nobility, the clergy, and even incorporated towns enjoyed certain exemptions that the crown dared not violate.

In the years leading to the Revolution, the people may indeed have considered French kings absolutists; but backstage, where the real decisions were made, these rulers had to take into account the demands of the groups and institutions that constituted the kingdom. This group included not only the nobility and the Church, but also powerful guilds and strong-willed members of the royal family. At times, the crown had to act against its own interests in order to appease one of these groups. For instance, when Louis XIV bowed to pressure exerted by the Church by revoking the Edict of Nantes that had protected the Huguenots, he did so despite the damage the decision would (and did) cause to the country's economy and international reputation.

On an economic level, the kings of this period were often weak, despite their so-called absolute power. The precarious financial situation of the crown was due essentially to the lack of a coherent system of taxation; it is difficult to be a despot when broke. W. H. Lewis notes that the nobility, clergy, and many government officials were totally exempt from taxation: "The whole fiscal system was in itself radically and incurably vicious; as a contemporary remarks, if the Devil himself had been given a free hand to plan the ruin of France, he could not have invented any scheme more likely to achieve that object than the system of taxation in vogue, a system which would seem to have been designed with the sole object of ensuring a minimum return to the king at a maximum price to his subjects, with the heaviest share falling on the poorest section of the population" (Lewis, 63).

Given these checks to absolutism—federalism, factionalism, the absence of a police force, and the near insolvency of the state—it is a wonder that the royal regimes were able to leave the amazing legacy that they did. On many levels, life in seventeenth- and eighteenth-century France improved considerably. New roads, ports, and canals were constructed and the pace of trade and communication accelerated accordingly. Theater and painting were supported by the crown and reached heights that still make them paradigms for artists. Students of the performing arts might get the impression that *all* French theater began in the seventeenth century!

The intellectual life during these centuries was flourishing. The main thinkers of the day often displayed political tolerance in their rational criticisms of contemporary judicial and moral abuses; new branches of knowledge became part of the canon; and new forms of scientific inquiry were fostered. A prime example of such intellectual advancement was the famous eighteenth-century "Encyclopedia," which would serve as a kind of theoretical preface to the French Revolution.

The Seventeenth Century

Louis XIII and Richelieu

The man who perhaps did the most to further royal absolutism was not himself a king, but rather a king's chief minister: Armand-Jean du Plessis, Duc du Richelieu (1585–1642). Like many noble families at the time, the Richelieus had been hard hit by the Wars of Religion. In order to maintain rights to a bishopric granted them by Henry III, a member of the family had to be consecrated as a bishop. That duty fell to young Armand-Jean when he was only twenty-two.

During Richelieu's young adulthood, France was in danger of resuming the religious conflict that had so profoundly unsettled the preceding century. Henry IV was assassinated in May 1610, when his successor, Louis XIII, was not yet ten years old. The regency under Queen Marie de Médici was corrupt, with various factions vying for favors and power. Furthermore, the Huguenot question remained largely unresolved. After Louis XIII came of age in 1614, his mother was implicated in two unsuccessful rebellions against the crown. As Marie de Médici's principal advisor, Richelieu managed to reconcile her to Louis, though her relationship with her king-son remained difficult throughout their lives.

Despite Richelieu's association with his troublesome mother, Louis XIII began to rely on him more and more for advice. By 1624 Richelieu had become his most valued minister. It has been suggested that Louis XIII was mentally unstable—at the very least, he was often ill and probably unable to concentrate on

Armand-Jean du Plessis, Cardinal and Duke de Richelieu, chief minister to King Louis XIII from 1624 to 1642.

matters of state—which created the conditions in which Richelieu could exert great influence. Given his importance, Richelieu was continually the object of court conspiracies, and he established a kind of personal security organization to root out conspirators. Though he sometimes dealt swiftly and severely with his enemies, as well as those he perceived to be enemies of the state, he has not gone down in history as a tyrant. In political principles, he seems to have shared the rationalism of the philosophers of his age. To this sensibility, he added a sense of morality that stemmed from his theological training. He abhorred disorder of any kind; for him, sin and civil disobedience were two sides of the same coin.

As for the Huguenots, it is quite possible that Richelieu would have tolerated them indefinitely, if they had not mounted a true political challenge to the crown: convincing Protestant England to wage war on France. The political situation was complicated by the fact that Spain pretended to help France combat the Huguenots, when in fact it was secretly funding them! Richelieu laid siege to the French Huguenot center of La Rochelle in 1628 and, after a year of hard fighting, took the city. In a decisive move, Richelieu immediately marched his army over the mountains in the dead of winter to quash the Spanish. Despite this victory, Richelieu was vulnerable at court. Marie de Médici was engaged in a veritable campaign against him, beseeching her son to dismiss him.

Louis XIII spent a day considering whether or not to follow his mother or Richelieu, and finally opted for the latter. As a result, his mother and the king's brother (who had formerly led an insurrection against the king) fled France. From that point on, Richelieu remained in favor at court, though he was forever in danger of losing Louis' support and his own life at the hands of court intriguers. In the very last months of his life (1642), his secret service uncovered a plot against him led by the king's favorite, Cinq-Mars, who was beheaded for his actions. Louis XIII died the following year.

Richelieu is known for having made France a leading European power. During his time at court, the Habsburg hegemony was defeated and Spain ceased to be a real threat to France. Richelieu, though no economic genius, nonetheless realized that international trade could increase national revenues and promoted industries that would create exportable products: glassmaking, tapestry, woolens, and silk, to name a few. He further oversaw the growth of French religious and trading missions throughout the world—Africa, the Middle East, the West Indies and the Americas—and took the first steps in building a fleet of sea-going vessels that would later be a bona fide navy. Last but not least, he was a serious patron of the arts and contributed some of his vast fortune to the Sorbonne. In addition, Richelieu founded the French Academy, a group of scholars and writers established to maintain standards of literary taste and correct usage of the French language. Over the three and a half centuries of its existence, the membership of the Academy—always limited to forty at any given time—has included many of the great names in French literature.

Louis XIV and the "Fronde"

Like his father, Louis XIV came to the crown young—he was only four years and eight months old—and, as in the preceding reign, the young king's mother was named regent. She, like Queen Marie de Médici before her, chose as her advisor a cardinal, Jules Mazarin. There end the similarities between Louis XIV and his father.

When Louis XIV was nine years old, the monarchy was confronted with a serious uprising known as "La Fronde" (the name of a sling used by naughty children in Paris). It is perhaps more appropriate to call the Fronde a civil war, for it lasted from 1648–1653 and included repeated armed conflicts. One main cause of the rebellion was the fact that certain privileged groups had had their influence weakened under Richelieu. These aristocrats did not like Mazarin any better; he was the target of fierce verbal attacks printed in pamphlets that were widely distributed in Paris. (This same tactic would be employed by members of another social class during the French Revolution, the next serious challenge to the monarchy.)

Basically, the proponents of the Fronde wished to limit the king's power to modify decrees. In 1648 the Parliament of Paris refused the crown's revenue measures, and civil war broke out in the city in January 1649. Although an uneasy peace treaty was ratified the following April, the Frondeurs were still not satisfied. Furthermore, they were divided amongst themselves. A cousin of the king, Condé, led one of the armed contingents of insurgents, but Mazarin's forces soundly defeated him—a defeat that led to the disintegration of the entire Fronde movement. Condé and many other nobles implicated in the affair fled to the Netherlands. By 1653, Louis XIV was able to enter Paris in a royal victory procession. The defeat of the Fronde had cast the nobility in a bad light by revealing their selfish interests. Henceforth the

Parliament was forbidden to interfere in royal administration, and the nobles lost their role in a check and balance system with the crown. In short, the Fronde's defeat increased the absolutism of the king.

Louis was quite young during the Fronde; he suffered from cold and hunger during those long years, and was undoubtedly shaped by the ordeal. Throughout his life Louis XIV trusted neither Paris nor the nobility. In the four decades leading up to the Fronde, nobles had, after all, started nearly a dozen civil wars and acts of armed dissension against the monarchy. One of the goals of Louis XIV's reign was to subdue the aristocracy, which he accomplished by keeping them at court and engaging them in gambling and other time-consuming but innocuous activities; in short, by encouraging them to live a life of dissipation. It could be argued that this implicit policy of de-activating the nobles ultimately had a negative effect on the nation by removing a large portion of the educated elite from politics. That may be true. But Louis XIV nonetheless found another group of men to advise him—a group decidedly *not* aristocratic, albeit educated, energetic, and ambitious.

Great Men and Great Projects under Louis XIV

Born into a merchant family, Jean-Baptiste Colbert (1619–1683) was one of these men. He received his lucky break when Mazarin, during his temporary exile from Paris during the Fronde, hired him as his personal agent in that city. Upon his return, Mazarin retained Colbert as his personal secretary at court until his death. With Mazarin's deathbed recommendation .

to Louis XIV, Colbert went on to serve the monarchy for the next twenty-five years.

Colbert continued Richelieu's encouragement of international trade and the development of a merchant and military navy. French industry prospered immensely. When tariffs to protect national industries were imposed on imports, however, France was drawn into a trade war with the Dutch. Protectionism extended to labor as well. French workmen were forbidden to work outside the country; French seamen could not, on pain of death, serve on non-French vessels.

Even harder to tackle than thorny trade issues was a chaotic system of taxation that was virtually medieval in conception. Colbert made great progress in curbing abuses—such as false titles of nobility to claim exemptions—and in supervising the collection of taxes. However, taxation would continue to be a problem throughout the following century.

One of the most famous of Louis XIV's tax agents was the Baron of Riquet (1604–1680), who became interested—and some say obsessed—with building a navigable canal across the south of France. In 1662 Riquet proposed the project to Colbert, who approved it and helped him negotiate with the provinces that the canal would cross. Riquet, a self-taught engineer, benefited from recent technological advances in the design and strengths of locks; their double-leaf metal gates made possible the construction of canals over long distances of varying elevation. Riquet was the first in France to use black powder in order to blast out tons of rock. He paved the way (so to speak) for the use of explosives in both railroad and road construction in later centuries. To judge by accounts left by his contemporaries, the baron was involved in the canal project in a very personal way. In fact, he ended up using his own vast fortune to fund the last stages of the project. Exhausted, he died on a construction site in Sète one year before the canal officially opened in 1681. The Canal du Midi, as it is now called, ran over 150 miles, and joined the Atlantic Ocean to the Mediterranean Sea. It was the greatest civil engineering project between the Roman era and the industrial revolution of the later nineteenth century.

The enthusiasm Riquet initially encountered at court for his building project reflected the generally positive attitude toward projects of such monumental proportions. This was, after all, the era of Versailles, the royal residence that cost nearly as much as a twentieth-century airport. While many French people of the time criticized the extravagance of this extensive castle during its construction, it did enhance the prestige of France and contributed to the absolutist, god-like image Louis XIV sought to promote. Versailles also isolated the king, his family, and the countless nobles who served and depended on the court. No longer did the king make periodic tours through his kingdom at large to meet his subjects. By the time of the French Revolution, the distance between the monarch and his subjects was virtually unbridgeable.

Louis XIV was not, however, distant from the business of ruling. Unlike his father, who was not predisposed to deal with the details of government, Louis XIV seemed to relish every aspect of the task. He attempted to concentrate all the administration of the monarchy in his own person—a formidable goal, to be sure. He personally supervised many matters: the establishment of a police force, the construction of Versailles, les Invalides, a military hospital, and other edifices and transporta-

113

Planned by the Baron Riquet in the 17th century, the Canal du Midi links the Mediterranean to the Atlantic Ocean. Pleasure crafts have now replaced the horse-drawn barges that used to transport goods, and bicyclists and walkers use the tow paths.

tion routes. It is a wonder that he found the time to attend theatrical performances, support artists, conduct various love affairs, and lead his country into a series of wars. By the age of forty, Louis had managed to defeat a coalition of Spain, the Holy Roman emperor, and the Dutch; to extend the border of France into Flanders, Lorraine, and the Franche-Comté; and to build a navy that rivaled that of England and the Netherlands. He was referred to as "The Sun King" with reason.

In 1682, when the king was forty-four, Versailles was ready to receive the royal family and court. The following year Colbert and the Queen died. It is generally thought that after the Queen's death, Louis XIV had but one woman in his life: Françoise d'Aubigné, the Marquise de Maintenon. What is not known, surprisingly, is exactly *when* the king married Mme de Maintenon, for the marriage was a closely guarded secret. Historians who attempt to determine the date often do so in order to argue that Mme. De Maintenon exerted great, and negative, influence over the king. There seems little ground to the claim that Mme de Maintenon played a role in the decision to revoke the rights of Huguenots; she had, in fact, been raised as a Huguenot during part of her childhood. Despite evidence that she created an atmosphere of dignity and piety around the king, for many years she was depicted in French textbooks as evil. At worst, Mme de Maintenon was ambitious. She had risen from poverty, and may even have been born in a debtors' prison. Once married to Louis, she used her influence to establish a convent school for impoverished aristocratic girls—such as she herself had once been. Louis XIV became more noticeably pious in the later years of his reign, undoubtedly under the influence of his wife.

Domestic and International Relations

Most historians consider Louis XIV's decline to have started in 1685 with the increased persecution of the Huguenots. The Assembly of the Clergy recommended that Huguenots be prevented from working as lawyers, librarians, printers, or hotel-keepers. These were all common professional activities of Huguenots, who were also often involved in commerce and industry. In October 1685, Louis XIV delivered a crushing blow to all members of the Reformed Religion, and by extension, to France itself: he revoked the Edict of Nantes that had guaranteed to the Huguenots their freedom to worship. The Reformed Church was consequently banished from France, and laws were passed making it a crime for a Huguenot (except for ministers) to leave the country, or for anyone to help a Huguenot escape. The penalty for these offenses was a life sentence in the dreadful galleys. ("Until the coming of the concentration camp," writes one observer, "the galley held an undisputed pre-eminence as the darkest blot on Western civilization" [Lewis 214]. Our detailed knowledge of life on the galleys at the time of Louis XIV is due largely to accounts written by Huguenots who survived to tell the tale.)

Despite these draconian measures, over 400,000 French Huguenots managed to emigrate to England, Germany, the Netherlands, and North America (especially Canada). This mass exodus created a vacuum in certain professional and technical domains that would be keenly felt during the first stages of industrialization. Huguenot emigration did not abate until the end of Louis' reign.

Four years after the revocation of the Edict of Nantes (1689), France entered into a conflict known as the "War of the Grand

Alliance," in which England, the Netherlands, and the Austrian Habsburgs joined forces against France. The war (1689–1697) revealed the extent of the rivalry between the Bourbons and the Habsburgs—a rivalry also fueled by the long-standing uncertainty as to which royal house would provide the next heir for the Spanish throne (the current Spanish king, the insane Charles II, being unable to produce children). The conflict turned into a war of attrition, with no decisive battles. The struggle was extremely costly to all sides, and the treaty that ended it brought no real resolution to the rifts between the Bourbons and the Habsburgs, or between the French and the English. In the course of the struggle, both England and Austria became serious counter forces to France.

In less than five years, these rifts erupted again in the War of the Spanish Succession (1701–1714). All the advantages that Louis XIV had gained in the first decades of his reign came close to being lost in this war. The treaty of Utrecht left French territory intact, but not its primacy on the international scene.

Louis XIV died at the age of seventy-seven (1715). In his *Age of Louis XIV*, Voltaire compares the French king to the Roman Augustus, saying that "his name can never be pronounced without . . . summoning the image of an eternally memorable age." Not everyone has been so laudatory; Louis XIV is sometimes depicted as a tyrant, divorced from his people and narrow-minded in his views.

French Literature in the Seventeenth Century

The seventeenth-century is referred to as the French "classical" age, characterized by a tendency toward order and delicacy in

117

language and art. Surprisingly enough, as the century dawned, nobles still spent most of their time on their estates hunting; many were illiterate, and most were considered uncouth. The move to refine manners and speech was intended to civilize the aristocracy. This was accomplished by Louis XIV's decision to draw large numbers of aristocrats to his court, where proper manners counted very much, as well as by the emergence of another milieu in which taste and sentiment were refined: the French "salon."

The "salons" of the seventeenth century were private gatherings, normally in the homes of prominent women. People who frequented salons included not only nobles, but also members of the growing bourgeoisie. The most highly valued personal attributes had less to do with class than with intelligence and wit. In these gatherings, a social ideal began to be developed—the "cultivated man" (*honnête homme*)—who was witty and elegant, well-spoken, and discreet. This ideal moved quickly from the realm of etiquette to literature. In salons, works in progress were often read aloud, and the audiences' reactions were sometimes taken into consideration by the authors as they continued to write.

The literature of this era is varied. The courtly ideals so popular in medieval literature were revived in some works, such as in Honoré d'Urfé's *L'Astrée*—a long pastoral novel written in the first years of the century. Later, many plays dealt with the contemporary scene. Molière's *Les Précieuses ridicules* (1659), for example, mocks the highly refined manners of salons as being hopelessly affected and artificial.

French Classical theater is dominated by two playwrights: Pierre Corneille (1606–1684) and Jean Racine (1639–1699), both of whom were great poets. Corneille produced a wide variety of plays over his forty-year career; he helped to raise the level of theatrical production in France and make it the envy of Europe. Corneille is particularly adept at depicting moral forces in conflict. His heroes display tremendous will power and energy in dealing with insurmountable odds, and are nothing if not admirable.

The male and female protagonists in *Le Cid* (1637) are heroes of this kind; they are faced with the conflict between passionate love and family honor. This play is noteworthy both for its role in the history of French tragedy, and for its own tumultuous history. It became the object of a literary debate that pitted Richelieu and his newly created *Académie Française* against the innovative playwright. The *Académie* criticized the play—and public performances of it were subsequently banned—for being implausible, defective on a moral level, and for not observing the dramatic unities (unity of place, time, and action). Richelieu's motives have never been clear. *Le Cid* is now considered the first example of French classical tragedy, a type of tragedy that is characterized less by technical rules (like the "unities") than by the heightened emotions displayed by the characters as they deal with wrenching dilemmas and reach—at least the true heroes— a moment of truth. *Le Cid* anticipated the tragedy of Racine, in whose work the moment of truth is most often a moment of painful self-realization.

Racine is reported to have told his son that Corneille's writing was "a hundred times more beautiful" than his own. Whether or not literary critics agree with Racine is less significant than the fact that he himself perceived Corneille as the father of French tragedy. That said, the world Racine creates is significantly different from Corneille's. Many of his plays are set in ancient times and many reflect the playwright's austere religious background and tendencies (known as Jansenism). For Racine, humans are controlled by passion, the strength and perversity of which they must constantly combat within themselves. There is a strong current of fatalism running through all Racine's plays; they present a series of events leading to a virtually inevitable catastrophe.

The eponymous heroine of *Phèdre* (1677) suffers from an incestuous passion that she cannot quell. *Phèdre* is considered among the most poetic of all Racine's tragedies. (It must be recalled that all of Racine and Corneille's plays were written in Alexandrine verse and meant to be "declaimed.") Like many seventeenth-century plays, it is still frequently staged throughout the world. *Phèdre* was Racine's last play before his premature retirement at the age of thirty-eight, after which he composed only two religious tragedies. Some believe that the play may reflect Racine's return to the principles of his youth; Racine's son claims that a serious religious experience was the cause of his father's retirement. It should be noted as well that the position Racine accepted upon his retirement—to write the official history of the reign of Louis XIV—offered a degree of financial security and prestige often lacking in the theater of his time. The theater was, in seventeenth-century France, a less dignified place to spend one's professional life than it has since become. The Church had frowned on theater for centuries, preventing actors and playwrights, for instance, from being buried in consecrated ground. It is unlikely that Racine was indifferent to the Church's negative view on theater.

The Eighteenth Century

The Enlightenment

The eighteenth century is often referred to as the Age of Reason because of the emphasis placed on rationality and its application in science, politics, ethics, and the arts. As previously noted, however, the importance of reason had already been emphasized by the Humanists of the early Renaissance period. This emphasis was particularly strong in their revival of texts from Antiquity and in their mode of scholarly inquiry—drawing conclusions solely on the basis of actual experience and research. The Enlightenment synthesized the insights of varied currents of thought: from the Humanists and Protestants of the fifteenth and sixteenth centuries, to the artists and scientists of the French Classical Age.

Like their predecessors, eighteenth-century thinkers wanted to free man from ignorance and superstition; they believed profoundly in the power of the mind to improve society. At the dawn of the century, Fontenelle wrote in an optimistic vein about the century before him, "a century that will become more enlightened day by day, so that all previous centuries will be lost in darkness by comparison" (1702). Thus, being "enlightened" meant emerging from the darkness of ignorance into the light of reason.

With this respect for reason, the Enlightenment melded a tendency toward passion that expressed itself in a veritable cult of sensibility (for instance in the development of the psychological novel); in a new, more favorable concept of nature (in the writings of Rousseau); and in a heightened social consciousness (in the philosophical and political essays of Voltaire and Montesquieu).

A representation of Paris in the 18th century. Note that the bridge in the background supports a row of buildings—a practice later forbidden.

The combination of reason and passion was volatile, and led—perhaps indirectly—to revolutionary fervor. Europe's most powerful monarchy was overthrown, and people began to envision democracy and social equality as realizable. But passionate fervor became excessive. The optimism engendered by the Enlightenment was clouded by the end of the century. It was not, however, extinguished.

Voltaire (1694–1778)

That Voltaire is considered one of the greatest French authors is rather surprising given the fact that relatively few of his abundant literary works are still read today. His fame is no doubt due to the life he led and the social causes he championed, as well as his wit, critical capacities, and morality. He was a tireless campaigner against tyranny and cruelty, and for clear thinking and enlightened rationality.

As a young man living in Paris under the regency (after the death of Louis XIV), Voltaire was a witty man-about-town whose epigrams were widely quoted in Parisian society. His first confrontation with authority was when he mocked the dissolute regent and was summarily locked up (in the Bastille prison) for over a year. In the years following his release, Voltaire's plays were well received and he was acclaimed as the successor of Jean Racine. Voltaire further aspired to be the epic poet of France, launching into a long poem that celebrates Henry IV for having ended the wars of religion.

But Voltaire became neither a great tragedian nor an epic poet. He was destined instead to a life of exile and opposition that began with a quarrel with a French noble. Voltaire was summarily beaten, taken again to the Bastille prison, and then transported to Calais, where he set out for London. He had long been interested in England as a country that tolerated freedom of thought, and he had learned English in order to read the philosophical works of John Locke. Now he seized his chance to meet the great men of English letters and philosophy: Alexander Pope, Jonathan Swift, and George Berkeley. Voltaire remained in England more than two years, and left that country determined to present it in a positive light to his compatriots. His *Lettres philosophiques* (1734) is a landmark in the history of ideas; it illustrates the effects of religious tolerance, and embodies the philosophy of the Enlightenment. Rather than trying to reach heaven through penitence, contends Voltaire, one should endeavor to assure happiness to the greatest number of people by devoting one's self to the progress of science and art.

The religious and political establishment in France was scandalized by Voltaire's book. It was not long before another warrant for Voltaire's arrest was issued. He sought refuge in the chateau of an intelligent and free-thinking woman, Mme du Châtelet, who was to be his almost constant companion for fifteen years. Mme du Châtelet was interested in science and is thought to have influenced Voltaire in that direction; they had a laboratory installed in the chateau. He continued to write on historical and social topics, often in the form of letters to various heads of state and thinkers throughout Europe. His volumes of letters are today considered a great monument of French literature.

For a time he acted as a counselor and agent for Frederick II of Prussia. As such, he returned to the good graces of the French court as well, where he was appointed historiographer and academician. However, the Catholic faction at court (including Louis XV) was not positively disposed toward the free-thinking Voltaire. He again retreated into hiding (after having made a caustic comment to Mme du Châtelet in English that was understood!). It was during this period that he discovered the literary form that was perhaps to best convey his ideas: the short tale or "conte." In *Zadig*, for instance, the persecuted hero begins to wonder if Providence is in fact looking after him. Given the trials that Voltaire underwent in his long life, it is tempting to read the tale as autobiographical.

The death of Mme du Châtelet in 1749 was a great blow to Voltaire. It is said that he would wander about at night calling her name. However, his grief diminished neither his activities nor the frequency of his travels. When Frederic II was enraged by a short work Voltaire wrote against a scientist in the Berlin Academy, Voltaire was forced to leave Prussia. He was subsequently held as a virtual prisoner in Frankfurt at an inn, being forbidden by Louis XV to approach Paris. After a year spent in the small border town of Colmar, Voltaire found asylum in Geneva; though, even there, some of his writings aroused the wrath of influential Calvinists.

The crux of this controversy was an article in Diderot's *Encyclopedia* on Geneva that Voltaire had inspired, though it was written by another "philosophe," Jean d'Alembert. In the article, Geneva was called upon to construct a theater, which local Calvinists had opposed on moral grounds. Jean-Jacques Rousseau then entered the fray, supporting the Swiss Calvinists in their opposition to theater. This event marks the definitive break between Rousseau and Voltaire, as well as the departure of Voltaire from Geneva.

Voltaire then purchased a property on the French-Swiss border so that he could evade the police of both countries. Again, he quarreled with local authorities, taking on the cause of Swiss workers (in fact, building a factory on his property in order to help them) and working toward the liberation of serfs in eastern France. (This last effort was not successful.) Voltaire intervened in a number of public scandals and trials throughout Europe. The social causes he most often promoted were religious tolerance, material prosperity for the greatest number, and respect for personal rights (the abolition of torture).

In the arts, Voltaire deplored the evolution of the public's taste in theater. He wanted a return to the kind of strict classicism that had made French tragedy great in the preceding century. But the mood in Europe was moving toward more melodramatic, "Shakespeare-like" theatrical spectacles, and even the great Voltaire could not stem the tide. It is, in fact, ironic that Voltaire's own early tragedies helped pave the way for the Romantic theater that would soon become popular.

Voltaire returned to Paris 1778, after an absence of nearly three decades, in order to direct a play. He was already ailing, and the pace of Paris life was perhaps too much for him; he died on May 30. Thirteen years later, during the French Revolution, his remains were transferred to the Panthéon, where the great thinkers and artists of France repose. One can only imagine what Voltaire would have written, however, had he lived to witness the more inhumane aspects of the French Revolution.

The ashes of Voltaire being transported to the Pantheon, where the illustrious of France repose.

Louis XV and Louis XVI

Voltaire's *The Century of Louis XIV* (1751) remains an important historical work because of the author's efforts to collect his information from as many witnesses as possible. Voltaire was himself a witness of the reign of the next Louis—Louis XV—but there was little love lost between this king and the forthright philosopher.

Louis XV was neither a son nor a grandson of Louis XIV, but rather a *great* grandson. Once again France was given a child-king, who ascended the throne at age five; and, once again, a regency was formed that created as many problems as it solved. Nineteenth-century historians tended to depict Louis XV as an ineffectual ruler who was unable to give direction to national policy. They claimed that during his nearly sixty-year reign, the crown's moral and political authority was diminished. Recent historians have recognized this king's strong points. The fact remains that Louis XV was not a king greatly loved by his people.

Like most kings, however, he was loved by a number of women. In his case, the officially recognized mistress became as renowned as the king himself. She was Jeanne-Antoinette Poisson, Marquise de Pompadour (1721–1764). This was a woman reared to be the wife of an important man. She could hold her own in any society and was acquainted with many influential men and writers. Madame de Pompadour replaced Louis XV's earlier mistress, who died in 1744, and acquired the title of marquise after moving to Versailles.

As the years passed, Madame de Pompadour exerted considerable influence at court, though perhaps less than her detractors claimed. She acted as a kind of personal secretary to the king, who was shy in public. One could argue that her relationship with the king was a collaboration, particularly in the realm of art and public works. She worked in close conjunction with her brother and the king to plan and have built a number of important monuments in Paris: the Ecole Militaire, the Place de la Concorde (then called the Place Louis XV), the Petit Trianon at Versailles, and a new wing for the palace of Fontainebleau. All kinds of art were supported by Louis XV upon the recommendation of Madame de Pompadour.

Upon Louis XV's death in 1774, his grandson became king. Louis XVI's reign has been the subject of countless studies, since it is inextricably bound to the French Revolution (discussed below). Louis XVI first perceived the growing revolutionary discontent as a product of aristocratic intransigence. Indeed, the aristocracy had been made stronger in the beginning of Louis XVI's reign when the powers of the Parlements, which had always supported the interests of the nobility, were restored. Louis XVI could have seized the opportunity to join the crown to middle-class reformers, but he chose instead to defend the privileges of the clergy and the nobility. In retrospect, this was a tactical error that further distanced the crown from the people.

Like the "Sun-King" (Louis XIV) of the seventeenth century, this last Louis never sought contact with the middle class, and thus did not seem to grasp the extent of popular dissatisfaction. By the time Louis XVI came to the throne, the middle class had grown considerably, and yet it was all but excluded from political power. Seemingly oblivious to the warning signs, Louis continued to pursue his personal hobbies—hunting, making locks, and doing masonry. When he finally realized the gravity of popular unrest, he tried to flee the country with his family, but was captured in eastern France and brought back in June 1791. At this juncture, the dignity of the crown had been seriously compromised. The situation then went from bad to worse.

Instead of implementing the constitution of 1791, as he had sworn to do, Louis XVI engaged in a series of plots in the hope that his regime would be saved by foreign intervention. The Austrians sent a warning that if the royal family was endangered, Paris would be destroyed. At news of this warning, the king's powers were temporarily suspended by the Legislative Assembly and the First French Republic was proclaimed (September 21, 1792). Two months later, Louis' secret counterrevolutionary schemes were unveiled—letters were discovered in a closet in the Tuileries Palace. On December 3, the decision was made to try the king for treason. The king was found guilty and condemned to death on January 18, 1793. He was guillotined three days later in the Place de la Révolution in Paris.

The French Revolution

It is a daunting task to describe succinctly the social unrest and complicated political maneuvers that characterize the tumultuous years 1787–1799. The French Revolution continues to be a popular object of analysis among historians, who rarely agree with one another as to the causes and implications of the conflicts. A number of factors, however, are cited as contributing directly to the fall of the monarchy.

First, there was a series of devastatingly bad harvests in France and, with no manageable system of grain distribution in the country, famine and peasant discontent were widespread. Starving peasants believed there was a conspiracy to sell French grain abroad. They were also becoming bolder in their refusal to tolerate the feudal system, in which they were highly taxed, poorly fed, and insufficiently represented in governing bodies. Second, the middle class—the growing bourgeoisie—had less political power than in other European countries. The commoners (the "Third Estate") had not met in an Estates-General since 1614.

Another important factor leading to the Revolution was, once again, the relative poverty of France in general. Added to chronic mismanagement of state finances and relative poverty, there was the large contribution that France made to help American revolutionaries in their effort to free themselves from English rule. Finally, the social and political reforms touted by the enlightened "philosophes" were quite widely read among middle-class reformers, who, in turn, published and distributed such ideas in inexpensive pamphlets. Revolution was in the air.

The situation became critical in the summer of 1789, when rumors of an aristocratic conspiracy were rampant, and the panic-stricken population took to the streets. On July 14, 1789, a mob arrived at the Bastille Prison and released the prisoners. Only seven men were then imprisoned there, but the act was nonetheless of great ideological importance for the revolutionaries. The medieval fortress was a symbol of the despotism of the French monarchy; here, the king could imprison anyone by issuing a "lettre de cachet," from which there was no recourse. The capture of the Bastille came to mark the symbolic end of the ancient régime; the date of its capture (not its demolition, which

People volunteering for service at the onset of the French Revolution.

The storming of the Bastille Prison, on July 14, 1789—the date chosen later for the French national holiday.

occurred some years later) was chosen as the French national holiday in 1880.

Revolutionary events were not limited to Paris. In the provinces, peasants rose against their local nobles. At this point, the aristocratic class and many bourgeois became frightened by the intensity and extent of the revolt. How could they calm the peasantry? On August 4, 1789, the National Constituent Assembly abolished the entire feudal regime and a much-hated tax. Later that month, the Declaration of the Rights of Man was written that proclaimed liberty, equality, and the right to resist oppression. At the same time, a decision was made to nationalize the lands held by the Church in order to pay off the public debt. (Numerous churches still bear the revolutionary inscription, "Liberty, Equality, Fraternity," over their portals; they are often the property of the municipality rather than of the Catholic Church.) To extend representation to the local level, France was divided into departments, districts, and communes to be administered by elected assemblies. Even judges were to be elected.

At this point in the Revolution, the Assembly was trying to create a monarchical regime in which the king would share power. Had Louis XVI embraced this idea, France might today have a very different government, something more like England's. However, that was not to be. Louis XVI closely followed the advice of his most conservative aristocratic counselors, and did everything he could to thwart the projects of the Assembly.

French nationalism was on the rise, fueled by armed conflict with the Austro-Prussian armies that were advancing toward Paris in the fall of 1792. Many French people felt, with reason, they had been betrayed by their king and the upper classes. In

EXECUTION DE LOUIS CAPET XVI.ᵉ DU NOM LE 21 JANVIER 1793.

The beheading of the King of France, Louis XVI, on January 21, 1793.

September the nobles and clergy imprisoned in Parisian prisons were massacred by revolutionary mobs. Volunteers swarmed into the French army, which was subsequently able to check the advances of the enemy; to occupy Belgium, the Rhineland, and Savoy; and to abolish the feudal system in those areas.

Despite these military victories, there was a growing rift among revolutionaries as to the desired extent of the war. Should France try to spread the revolution throughout Europe as proposed by the Girondins (members of the National Convention from southwestern France)? Or should it rather limit all activity to France as the Montagnards believed? The Montagnards were led by the famous Robespierre, who was a champion of the cause of the lower classes and wanted a greater role in government for them.

This difference in opinion was rendered moot by a series of military defeats that brought the Prussians nearly to the gates of Paris. The Girondin leaders were driven out of the National Convention, and the Montagnards adopted radical social measures. They taxed the rich and confiscated all properties held by the aristocrats and bourgeois who had fled the country, made education compulsory, and established a kind of social welfare system for the very poor.

From the fall of 1793 to the following summer, the Committee of Public Safety, of which Robespierre was the most prominent member, decided to take harsh measures against people they suspected of being counterrevolutionaries. This was a broad group including those both on the left and the right: aristocrats, clergy, and even hoarders. The period is rightly called the "Reign of Terror." The Committee exerted true dictatorial control over French government; for example, it ensured that a law was passed in the National Assembly suspending a person's right to public trial and to legal counsel. Another law, introduced by a physician named Joseph-Ignace Guillotin, required that all state executions be carried out by beheading. Strangely enough, Guillotin's law was inspired by social and humane concerns: that decapitation would no longer be a "privilege" of the aristocratic class, and that the ordeal would be as painless as possible. (The guillotine was last used in 1977, four years before capital punishment was outlawed in France.) The official death toll by execution during the Reign of Terror stands at seventeen thousand (including Robespierre himself when he fell out of favor). Many others undoubtedly died incarcerated in terrible conditions, or were killed without trial (or record). A period of reaction—sometimes referred to as the "White Terror," for its royalist leanings—followed the Terror; it was particularly strong in the west and southeast of the country. When Royalists tried to take Paris in the fall of 1795, they were defeated by a young Napoleon Bonaparte. Thus began a new regime, the Directory.

The Napoleonic Wars (1795–1815)

The Directory, run by an executive group of five, together with two legislative chambers, might have fared well had a series of wars not exacerbated the friction between revolutionaries and counterrevolutionaries throughout Europe. These wars were essentially between France—whose military was under Napoleon's leadership—and various alliances of European powers. For a brief time, there was French hegemony over most of Europe.

Although the French ostensibly undertook these wars to spread the liberalizing message of the French Revolution, they ended up engaging in aggression with the aim of increasing their own territory and influence.

Most of the countries that Napoleon occupied or conquered were established as "sister republics" modeled on Revolutionary France. In 1798 and 1799, the French established the Helvetic, Roman, and Parthenopean republics in Switzerland; the Papal States; and Naples, respectively. The English, on the other hand, proved harder to conquer. Rather than try to invade in England, Napoleon chose to occupy Egypt in order to threaten the British presence in India. In the decisive Battle of the Nile in 1798, a French squadron was destroyed by the English under Horatio Nelson. At this point, a powerful alliance—Austria, Russia, Turkey, and Great Britain—was formed to check the progress of Napoleon. The coalition managed to drive back French forces, and Napoleon returned to France.

Once on his home turf, Napoleon abolished the Directory and proclaimed himself the "first consul" of France. This is known as the famous—or infamous depending on one's point of view—"coup d'état of 18 Brumaire," so named because of its date on the revolutionary calendar (November 9, 1799). The expansionist wars, however, were far from over. In 1800 Napoleon won an important victory over Austria that confirmed France's role as the dominant power on the continent. By 1805 another coalition formed; this time it allied Britain, Russia, and Austria. After a number of military encounters, France was again the victor. All of continental Europe was thus under the control of the French, or allied to France by treaty—except for Portugal, Sweden, Sardinia, and Sicily.

Napoleon's luck did not change until his invasion of Russia in 1812. The Russians well understood Napoleon's military strategy and decided to beat him at his own game. They simply withdrew and let Napoleon's troops enter Russian territory as the fall season was approaching. The French army was unable to win the only full-scale engagement of the war, at Borodino in September, and Napoleon was forced to retreat many hundreds of miles along a route that was depleted of any means of sustenance for his massive army. The temperatures dropped to −30°F (−35 °C), and five hundred thousand men were subsequently lost.

Following this stunning defeat, Napoleon's allies began to desert him. He was exiled to the island of Elba; however, in the space of a year, he was nonetheless able to rally a new army. Another coalition was formed among his adversaries, and the last Napoleonic war began. This is the moment when, as the saying goes, "Napoleon met his Waterloo." As in Russia, he was unable to surprise the enemy. In this case, he could not prevent his enemies from attacking from two fronts. Two separate offensive lines—the Dutch and English, and the Prussians—invaded France. Napoleon abdicated on June 22, 1815. The monarchy was restored in the person of Louis XVIII.

CHAPTER FIVE

CHANGE, CHANGE, AND MORE CHANGE: THE NINETEENTH CENTURY

Romanticism

Romanticism was a cultural movement that spread through Europe in the late eighteenth and nineteenth centuries and profoundly influenced literature, painting, music, architecture, and politics for many years. Jean-Jacques Rousseau (1712–1778) was one of the most influential precursors of Romanticism in France; he rejected aristocratic elegance, inspired a veritable cult of nature, and revived religious sentiment in a public that questioned Church dogma. The trend toward more accessible and personal forms of expression was especially popular among the middle class. Indeed, the success of Romanticism was clearly linked to the rise of the bourgeoisie in the nineteenth-century economy.

Romanticism was fueled by a spirit of opposition to the order and rules of Classicism, and to the rationality and materialism of Enlightenment thought in general. Romanticism exalted creative spirit over adherence to formal rules, emotion over reason, and the senses over the intellect. It sought spiritual truth through the imagination and through experiences considered transcendent, mysterious, or exotic. The literary and plastic arts reflected these interests. Eugene Delacroix, for example, painted a number of exotic images from the Arabian culture he saw in North Africa. Romantics were often drawn to studies of folk culture and of the Middle Ages, both of which became objects of scholarly historical research.

All of this seems very far from politics, but in fact, the Romantic Movement in the nineteenth century had a profound political effect. It brought together people with similar liberal views who were, for the most part, opposed to the established political order. In the first decades of the nineteenth century, Victor Hugo was called "the most powerful mind of the Romantic movement." Little did people know then that his life would span nearly the entire century, and that his writings would provide future generations with a mirror—perhaps not without distortion, but in any case *immense*—of the political and aesthetic tendencies of nineteenth-century France.

The Nineteenth Century as Lived by Victor Hugo (1802–1885)

Early in his life Hugo was, like the nineteenth century itself, torn between royalist tendencies and veneration for the republican ideals of the French Revolution. His mother was a confirmed royalist, while his father was a general in Napoleon's army. They were often at odds and often lived in separate cities. How could these apparently incompatible points of view be reconciled? This was something that the nineteenth century had to sort out. So did Hugo.

Hugo's earliest works reflect the influence of his mother's royalist tendencies; he was, in fact, accorded a pension by King Louis XVIII (1814–1824). In the late 1820s, Hugo became a more passionate and provocative opponent of the restored monarchy, especially when Charles X (1824–1830) took a decidedly reactionary turn. (Charles X increased censorship, restored power to the clergy, and even imposed the death penalty for certain "sacrileges.") Hugo's renewed defense of freedom and his poetic depictions of a very idealized Napoleon brought him into a circle of liberal thinkers in Paris, who, in the current climate of general repression, tended to band together. More than one of these young Romantics must have identified with a character in Hugo's play, *Hernani*, who was a noble outlaw at war with society.

When a constitutional king, Louis-Philippe, was brought to power in the July 1830 Revolution, people such as Hugo found a way to reconcile the legacy of the French Revolution—republican principles of representation—with the need for a strong national leader. To celebrate the event, Hugo composed the first of many political poems he would write over the years.

However, France's monarchy became increasingly repressive in the 1840s. Liberals, many now inspired by new socialist theories, longed for change once more. Change came in the form of the revolution of 1848, and the proclamation of the Second Republic. Hugo was elected to the National Assembly, but soon became disillusioned. After the coup d'Etat of 1852 and the establishment of the Second Empire, Hugo fled the country and did not return to his homeland for two decades—until France had been defeated in the Franco-German War in 1871, and the Third Republic had been proclaimed. He was again elected to the National Assembly, but resigned the following month. When he died in 1885, thousands of people walked in his funeral cortège. For many French, he remains a symbol of republicanism, and a national hero. (Nearly every French city has a street named after him!)

Several of Hugo's literary works are renowned throughout the world; the two most translated are *Notre Dame de Paris* (*The Hunchback of Notre Dame*, 1831), and *Les Misérables* (the title, meaning "the wretched," is usually not translated in English). The interest we have in Hugo's characters lies less in their intimate passions and their burning conscience than in the world they inhabit. Hugo's heroes are inextricably tied to their historical context and to events that they cannot fully comprehend but which determine their existence and any meaning they can derive from it.

In *The Hunchback of Notre Dame*, society is condemned for its brutal treatment of outcasts (a deformed man and a gypsy woman). The public consciousness of Hugo's audience was moved by the spectacle; readers undoubtedly saw parallels between Quasimodo's world—medieval France—and their own. Thirty years later, Hugo scored another immediate success with *Les Misérables*. Like Quasimodo, the protagonist of *Les Misérables*, Jean Valjean, is a victim of society. He becomes an outcast when he is sentenced to nineteen years of hard labor for having stolen a loaf of bread. Valjean eventually escapes and becomes an outstanding citizen; but over the years, he is relentlessly tracked by an obsessive police detective. Valjean ends up sacrificing himself for his adopted daughter, when, during the tumultuous Paris uprising of 1832, he carries his daughter's lover through the city's sewers with the detective in pursuit. This is the

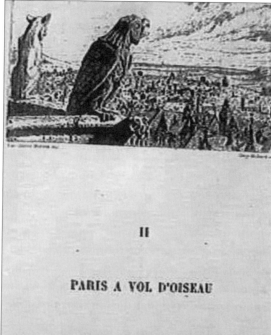

II

PARIS A VOL D'OISEAU

Nous venons d'essayer de réparer pour le lecteur cette admirable église de Notre-Dame de Paris. Nous avons indiqué sommairement la plupart des beautés qu'elle avait au quinzième siècle et qui lui manquent aujourd'hui; mais nous avons omis la principale, c'est la vue de Paris qu'on découvrait alors du haut de ses tours.

C'était en effet, quand, après avoir tâtonné longtemps dans la ténébreuse spirale qui perce perpendiculairement

A page from an illustrated edition of Victor Hugo's Notre Dame de Paris *(1831). The title of the chapter is "A Bird's-eye view of Paris."*

story of man's battle with evil that provides us not only with a larger-than-life hero, but also with a panorama of nineteenth-century French life—the criminal underworld, the low-paid working class, the well-off bourgeois—and the events that defined the era (for example, the Battle of Waterloo is described over an entire chapter).

From Romanticism to Realism

Hugo's *The Hunchback of Notre Dame* reflects and perpetuates the great popularity of the historical novel in the first decades of the nineteenth century. It is perhaps natural that what was perceived as a "new" era after the Revolution would be ushered in with a "new" way of depicting the world. As influential as Romanticism was in nineteenth-century thought, an alternative way of perceiving and describing the world came on the scene in the mid-century: realism.

Honoré de Balzac set about to create a truly encyclopedic portrayal of the society in his *Comédie humaine*; and the painter Courbet translated this same aesthetic to canvas. In 1857 Champfleury published a kind of manifesto of realism that called for the representation of ordinary people in art, rather than exceptional figures; and Gustave Flaubert published *Madame Bovary*, a novel that presents a brutal picture of an unhappy, bourgeois wife who has been nurtured on romantic novels through her youth, and for whom reality is disappointing. The brothers Goncourt were also important realist writers whose novels explored various social milieus and relations among classes. In their cogent but controlled social critique, these authors embody the tenets of literary realism: objective detachment mixed with concerned engagement.

An offshoot of realism was naturalism—a movement more explicitly aimed at a faithful, indeed scientific, depiction of reality. As these trends began influencing artists and writers, politicians were also becoming more engaged in social issues, especially those emerging from the industrial revolution.

The Industrial Revolution

The term "revolution" commonly used to describe the tremendous economic and industrial changes that occurred in Europe in the nineteenth century can be misleading. These changes did not really happen with the suddenness of a revolution. In fact, modes of commercialization were beginning to change in the eighteenth century. Peasants near towns and cities were selling the food they raised to urban residents; and some rural domestic manufacturing (of thread, cloth, tools) was being sponsored by city merchants. These rural people had what their parents had not: available cash that enabled them to purchase commercially made goods. This increased the wealth of city manufacturers, who in turn developed new tastes for new products.

Economic prosperity was furthered in the nineteenth century by an increase in population. In some areas, there was an increase of over 100 percent, which was in part due to the relative absence of war and epidemic diseases—with the exception of the devastating cholera outbreak that swept through France

147

around 1832. The bad side of the population boom was that many people were unable to continue earning a living as their fathers had done, whether on a farm or as rural craftsmen. The good side was that these people were available to fill openings in urban factories.

Factory work was more plentiful than ever in this age of steam, gas, and electricity—truly revolutionary forms of power that fueled both manufacturing and transportation. Great advances in chemistry brought forth a plethora of new products: pharmaceuticals, perfumes, and fertilizers. Some that had previously been luxury items—chocolate, coffee, tea, and sugar—became available to the masses through changes in production. (Making sugar from beets was a French invention dating from 1810.)

Improvements in the fabrication of paper and the invention of the rotary press (1867) made it possible to print in one hour as many pages as the older presses had printed in three months. Increased production of newspapers, and their low cost, meant that many more working-class people had access to them. This outlet, in part, contributed to the increased political engagement of people of this class, especially in the cities where the gap between rich and poor was growing ever wider.

From the mid-century on, newspapers, tracts, and pamphlets popularized socialist and utopian ideas. The term *socialistes* referred generally to those who felt that the ideals of the French Revolution—freedom and equality—still had not been realized. It must be noted that one change brought about by the Revolution, the abolition of trade associations, might have actually worsened the condition of the working classes because it deprived them of organized associations with articulate spokesmen to champion their causes. Nineteenth-century workers were often isolated and unable to take steps to improve their lot in the absence of effective labor laws. Women and young children worked long hours with no reprieve.

Women working in a shoe factory at the turn of the century.

Social Unrest: From Monarchy to Republic to Empire

The government under King Louis Philippe (1830–1848) had shown itself oblivious to the demands for reform issuing from broad sectors of the population. Suffrage was still limited to the relatively wealthy individuals who were able to pay a poll tax. On February 22, 1848, a gathering of reformists was banned, and people took to the streets in Paris. The night after some fifty protesters had been killed, barricades went up all over the city. Fierce street fighting filled the next days, and Louis-Philippe finally abdicated on February 24th. He conferred the crown on his grandson. But by now, it was too late. The "Chambre des députés" (legislature) was dissolved by its members and a provisional government was established.

The more radical of the social reformers pushed the legislature further to the left than ever before. The most astounding act was the declaration of universal manhood suffrage, which increased the electorate from 200,000 to 9,000,000. The legislators also issued a right-to-work declaration, and established emergency relief agencies called "ateliers nationaux." However, when the new electorate went to the polls, it was clear that the majority of voters supported more moderate or even conservative candidates. The resulting assembly—the first of the newly formed Second Republic—was not willing to launch into what they considered risky social experiments.

The result of the move to the right by the lawmakers was, again, fighting in the streets of Paris, as workers joined with students and artisans to express their disagreement. A general,

Cavaignac, established order by killing some 1,500 rebels and arresting over 10,000 others.

Despite the way in which the reform movement was crushed, it did not wither away. A number of legislative reforms were maintained: universal male suffrage, and the election of a president, rather than the restoration of monarchy. The constitution written at the outset of the Second Republic was the most democratic in Europe. Louis-Napoleon, a nephew of the Emperor Napoleon I, was elected president by a landslide; though in the next elections, the moderate republicans—the framers of the liberal constitution—were voted out of office in favor of politicians who were more radical on both the left and the right.

During the following two years, President Louis-Napoleon allowed the government to slip in a decidedly conservative direction: for instance, a third of the French were denied the vote, the press and the right to assemble were limited, and education was controlled almost entirely by the Church. Louis-Napoleon may have been courting conservatives because he wanted a constitutional amendment allowing him to run for a second term as president. When his efforts failed, he led a coup d'État in 1851 that led to the arrest of numerous politicians and to a new constitution. The streets once again filled with protesters; several hundred lost their lives and thousands were arrested. In 1852, Louis-Napoleon was named emperor. A plebiscite conducted in the wake of the event shows that an amazing 97% of the voters supported the move.

The record of Emperor Napoleon III, as Louis-Napoleon was henceforth called, is mixed. Like modern politicians, he was very concerned with public opinion and used propaganda to influence it. Although as president he had allowed the legislature to move toward the right, as emperor he instigated a number of reform-minded policies. Among them were mutual aid societies that brought together employees and employers, and the construction of housing for workers. Freedom of assembly was granted in 1868, and restrictions on the press were lightened. However, these reforms may have come too late to quell the country's general dissatisfaction in the 1860s. Opposition to Napoleon III, especially among the middle class, grew stronger.

In these years, the opposition was strengthened not only by economic distress, but also by certain failures in Napoleon III's foreign policy. Relations with Prussia were coming to a crisis point. In the elections of 1869, the opposition party made a very strong showing. The emperor tried to mitigate the damage by appointing a liberal politician as prime minister, and by informing England and Prussia that France would disarm. The Prussian leader Bismark refused to cooperate, and war broke out in the summer of 1870.

Napoleon III, by this time physically ailing and probably emotionally drained, tried to die on the battlefield . . . but failed. He was forced to surrender to Bismark on September 2, 1870, and was subsequently deposed. Here began the Third Republic, which was to last until World War II (1940).

The Commune and the Dreyfus Affair

The decision by the National Assembly to surrender to the Prussians was not accepted by all the French. A significant number of Parisians, fearing that the conservative Assembly would vote to restore the monarchy, opposed the decision. Conflict in Paris broke out on March 18, 1871, when government troops, under orders from Versailles, began to disarm the National Guard—a contingent comprised largely of workers who had defended Paris against the Prussians. The head of the provisional Versailles government, Adolphe Thiers, was forced to call back his forces in the face of opposition by the defenders of Paris.

When Parisian municipal elections occurred a week later, leftist leaders won and formed a government that they called the "Commune." The members of this group included those who ascribed to the ideals of the French Revolution, socialists who supported a loose confederation of communes throughout France, and more radically inclined socialists who called for revolution. Indeed, at this point, there were similar "communes" in other large French cities—Lyon, Saint-Etienne, Marseille, and Toulouse—and Prime Minister Thiers, supported by conservative European leaders, felt it imperative to put down all these movements.

In Paris, the repressive action against the communards was swift and brutal. Far more died in May 1871 than in the entire Franco-Prussian War, or even the French Revolution itself. The death toll for the Paris Commune is placed at around 30,000 communards and some 900 government soldiers. Over 50,000 communards were arrested and sentenced either to death or to exile in New Caledonia, a French colony off the coast of Australia. Studies of the event refer to it as a true massacre. Communards defended their neighborhoods behind makeshift barricades. Witnesses reported French soldiers lining up insurgents against walls and executing them without trial.

The proclamation of the "Commune" in 1871.

Witnesses also reported the active participation of women on the barricades, and their presence among the executed and deported. Over one hundred women were said to have erected and defended the barricade at the Place Blanche; and when it fell, so did they in the general bloodbath of that week. "The attitude of women during the Commune," wrote one contemporary, "was a source of admiration among foreigners and exasperation among the Versailles forces."

The Commune continues to be an ideologically charged issue for obvious reasons. For many years, the subject was given little or no attention in school textbooks. Along with the Commune, the end of the nineteenth century saw another conflict that also pitted the political "left" against the "right," and that profoundly marked French social history for many years. This was the Dreyfus affair, a trial for treason that lasted a dozen years.

Alfred Dreyfus (1859–1935), the son of a wealthy Jewish manufacturer, was a French army officer accused of having sold military secrets to the Germans. In 1894 he was convicted and sentenced to a life term. Articles in the right-wing French newspapers gave vent to anti-Semitic hostility against all French Jews; while articles in left-leaning papers started to express doubts about Dreyfus' guilt. These doubts were increased first by Lieutenant Colonel Picquart's discovery that the handwriting on a piece of incriminating evidence at Dreyfus' trial was in fact that of a certain C. F. Esterhazy, and secondly by Picquart's removal from office after his revelation.

When Esterhazy was acquitted of the charge of forgery and Picquart arrested, the novelist Emile Zola wrote an open letter in a prominent newspaper that accused the army of covering up its unjust conviction of Dreyfus under order of the Ministry of War. At this point in the scandal, the French split into two distinct camps. Those defending Dreyfus—known as Dreyfusards— tended to be wary of the military, and to espouse the freedom of the individual against state authority. The anti-Dreyfusards included those who were nationalistic and did not want the French army discredited, as well those who were more radically conservative and saw the whole affair as an example of the dangers of international socialism and Jewry.

The Dreyfusards called for a new trial for Dreyfus, while the anti-Dreyfusards pressed the government to charge Zola with libel for his outspoken article. As this debate raged, anti-Semitic riots occurred throughout France. New events in the case complicated matters further. The man who had supposedly discovered the letter that incriminated Dreyfus ended up confessing that he had forged them, and shortly thereafter committed suicide. Esterhazy fled the country. Dreyfus was given a new trial in a military court, but was again found guilty. Zola was also tried and found guilty of libel. The president of France quickly pardoned Dreyfus, but he was not cleared of the charges by a civilian court until 1906.

France, with its tradition of distinct political camps dating from the Revolution, was more polarized than ever over the Dreyfus affair. The effects of the animosities between the two camps made themselves felt well into the twentieth century. Although some loudly condemned anti-Semitism, the Dreyfus affair also brought latent racist feelings to the surface where they were given expression in written form.

Press coverage of Zola's trial in the Dreyfus affair (February 12, 1898).

"Peasants into Frenchmen"

The Commune and the Dreyfus affair were dramatic events that profoundly marked the late nineteenth and early twentieth centuries. However, they did not mark all the French in the same way or at the same time. Clearly, Parisians were more aware of these events and their effects than were their counterparts in the provinces.

What were the formative events in the lives of the many French who lived and worked outside urban centers during the nineteenth century? This is a question that an increasing number of historians are asking, though the answers are harder to discover in the diverse and often undocumented history of rural France. One thing, however, seems clear: significant changes occurred in the lives of French peasants in the late nineteenth and early twentieth centuries.

In his *Peasants into Frenchmen: the Modernization of Rural France, 1870–1914*, Eugen Weber notes the radical change that French villages underwent in these years: "Material conditions, mentalities, political awareness, all underwent massive alterations, a sort of precipitation process wholly different from the rather gradual evolutions or sporadic changes that accumulate to make what we describe as a period of history. Historical change rushing in headlong carried [French villages] not from one historical period to another, but into a new age of mankind—an altogether different form of civilization." Weber begins his study by describing the conditions of rural life before the onset of such changes; peasants in the mid-nineteenth century lived much as they had in centuries long past, using the same (or hardly improved) farming techniques, and running their families and village life according to traditional rules. All this was to change in a relatively short period of time.

Weber's title, "Peasants into Frenchmen," suggests that peasants were in some way transformed into "Frenchmen" in the nineteenth century. What does it mean for a peasant to be considered, or to consider himself, French? Feeling oneself to belong to a national group implies sharing a common history and experiences with the members of that group. Until peasants communicated and traded with people outside their villages, and had contact with ideas coming from elsewhere in the country, they were not able to conceive of themselves as French. Such exposure to others was made possible by the development of roads, railroads, and other means of transportation and communication.

Roads and Railroads

In the early nineteenth century, France had quite a few long-distance roads. In many cases, they were constructed on roadbeds built by the Gauls or the Romans, and joined cities that had existed for many centuries. Nineteenth-century armies (and tax collectors) marched along the same roadways that their predecessors had traveled.

Yet, the great majority of peasants did not live along the existing roads; and no secondary road system was built or even planned until late in the century. In some remote areas, there were few practicable roads before the mid-twentieth century. The road construction that was undertaken during Napoleon I's Empire (1804–1815) was not motivated by the needs of common people, but rather by the necessity of moving troops over long distances. For their part, peasants used footpaths that crisscrossed the countryside from house to house and village to village. More often than not, these paths could not be traveled only on foot, horse, or mule. As a result, rural people preferred to trade their goods close to home rather than carry them on their backs over long distances. The barter system was widespread in the French countryside, except in areas close to a large town or a large highway. Any produce that could not be traded very locally, or transported without spoiling to a town market, was not grown in areas without roads. Thus, in many fertile areas, farmers did not attempt to grow fruit as a cash crop. They simply had no way to market it outside their own communities.

At first, the advent of railroads did not greatly alter this situation. Railroads were initially built according to the same principles that governed road planning; that is, according to the needs of urban areas and the military. There were very few branch lines serving small towns and villages. Larger cities lucky enough to possess a rail line were connected to Paris, not to cities of a size comparable to their own. The decisions of railroad officials as to where to lay the line had serious demographic consequences. Weber reports that, "between 1866 and 1936 rural communes without a railway station in a zone 15 km on either side of the Paris-Lyons-Mediterranean line lost almost one-quarter of their population, while those with a station gained 1,645,373 inhabitants."

Secondary roads tended to be constructed in concert with train stations, so that the development of secondary roads and railroad lines occurred almost simultaneously. As the nineteenth century drew to a close, common people gradually gained greater access to roads that allowed them to travel and transport their goods in wagons. The impact of this change should not be underestimated. At last, a much greater number of French peasants were able to participate in what had become a truly *national* market; at last, the prosperity of the urban industrial centers flowed into the country. The new roads and railroads in France also brought cultural capital—newspapers, books, traveling theaters, and musical groups—to a rural population progressively more open to influences from outside their regions.

Teaching French to the French

The Third Republic made primary education in France compulsory, secular, and *free* in the 1880s. State-administered and funded education was not, however, a new concept at this point. Fifty years before (1833), Minister of Public Instruction François Guizot had established certain basic requirements to promote primary education in France: communes (usually somewhat smaller than U.S. counties) or groups of small communes had to have at least one primary school, and every *département* (similar to a U.S. state) had to establish a training school for teachers. As a result, mid-century France had over 60,000 schools attended by some three million children. Even before Guizot placed a high priority on education, the revolutionaries at the close of the eighteenth century had set out to educate the rural masses; they were particularly interested in spreading the use of the French language in order to make proper "citizens" of the country's inhabitants. Nevertheless, they faced tremendous obstacles in training and paying teachers, as well as in getting them into the hinterlands of rural France. Only with the laws of 1881–85 were these barriers overcome. The government of Jules Ferry (premier from 1880–81 and 1883–85) was willing to advance the funds necessary to train and pay teachers for rural schools. The road and railway systems to join teachers to students were already well under way.

One of the leaders of education in the 1880s, Ferdinand Buisson, succinctly stated the main pedagogic goal when he declared that "teaching French, our beautiful and noble mother tongue, is the chief work of the elementary school—a labor of patriotic character." In this view, Buisson hardly differed from the revolutionaries of the preceding century. It would be over fifty years, however, before most schoolchildren arrived for their first day of school with French as their mother tongue.

Many children living in rural France up until the 1920s (and some until World War II) rarely heard the French language before going to school. Some spoke other established languages such as Flemish, Breton, Basque, or Alsatian (German). In southern France from Bordeaux to Marseilles, most people spoke various dialects of Occitan, an ancient language with a distinguished literary history. Local "patois"—which most dictionaries define as "provincial" or "uneducated" speech—were, and still are, spoken in many parts of France.

Nineteenth-century peasants were attached to their patois as many people are attached to the language their mothers spoke. The irony in France is that French was considered the national language more than a century before it was truly a "mother tongue" for the majority of its citizens. Primary school is what changed French into a true mother tongue for all, but it was a very long and painful process. Children were punished for speaking patois within the walls of the schoolhouse. Testimonies from people still living today convey the injustice some felt at being wrenched from their mother tongue and forced to use a language whose utility they did not necessarily perceive. Indeed, here appears the crux of the matter: only when peasants felt that knowing French was in their self-interest, and important for the future of their children, did the French start to make serious progress toward becoming a truly "national" language. This happened to different people at different times.

One effect of the legislation of the 1880s was that young girls were henceforth required to go to school, whereas before there had been neither the funds nor the inclination to send girls to secular elementary schools. Without education, girls remained monolingual, speaking only patois with their husbands, children, and neighbors. Once girls began to master French, they could—if they chose—speak to their own children in that language. In these cases, French became a true "mother tongue."

In the village where I live, one of my neighbors, a woman in her early seventies, is clearly proud to say that she spoke only French to her five children, thinking it best for their own development. On the other hand, she continued to speak in patois to her husband and contemporaries, as she still does. Most people here over the age of sixty still speak patois to one another, and French to anyone from outside the commune. These people learned French as a foreign language at the local school, like another neighbor whose grandfather insisted he be sent to school two years earlier than other children so that he would learn French, since his parents and relatives all spoke only patois.

What must these people think when they hear that Occitan—the language they were punished for speaking in school fifty years ago—is now being taught in the same school as a foreign language! Needless to say, some children today (mine included) don't see the purpose of learning Occitan when their parents and friends all speak French, just as many of their nineteenth-century ancestors saw little sense in learning French in their Occitan world. As the French frequently say: "The more things change; the more they stay the same."

CHAPTER SIX

WAR AND PEACE
THE TWENTIETH CENTURY

Overview

The Industrial Revolution of the nineteenth century—with its steam power, railroads, and manufactured consumer goods—was only one stage in the modernization of Western Europe. The transformation of society brought about by twentieth-century inventions and discoveries was even more spectacular. However, progress has two faces, only one of which is positive. The technological advances of the century—automobiles, electricity, mass communications, petrochemicals, aeronautics, subatomic physics—ushered in new prosperity but also devastating forms of warfare and oppression. Industrial progress brought material abundance to many French, but it pushed others to the margins of society.

Change occurred in the twentieth century at a hallucinating pace. Photographs taken around the First World War (1917) are scarcely different from those taken half a century earlier. We see men in top hats and women in voluminous long dresses; horse-drawn carriages in cities; shepherds with their flocks. Twenty years later, the changes were considerable: skirts had been shortened and motorized cars filled city streets, though shepherds

Illustration from a magazine article on war refugees (January 12, 1918). Note that the style of dress is barely distinguishable from 19th-century fashion.

This drawing from a popular magazine (May 13, 1933) shows the great changes in clothing that occurred in the second decade of the 20th century.

Even in Paris, with more paved roads than elsewhere, most "carriages" were still drawn by horses in 1910.

Two decades later, not only were cars common, but women were driving them!

continued their traditional work. Mass culture was well on its way as the middle class grew in size and prosperity. Laws were enacted in the 1930s that limited the workweek to forty hours and required employers to pay for vacations. Nevertheless, these enlightened changes could not prevent France from being drawn into another world war—called by many French the "War of 1939"—that would demoralize the country for years to come. In a terrible twist of fortune, the man responsible for much of the social legislation of the late 1930s, Léon Blum, was himself deported by French authorities to a German concentration camp during the war—along with thousands of other French citizens of Jewish origin.

Half a century after the war, the professional and personal life of most French people has changed considerably. More French have moved to urban areas, often outside their native regions and far from the extended family that used to form the organizing principle of French life. In 1939 nearly one-third of the total population lived and worked in rural areas, whereas in the 1990s barely five percent did. This small minority of farmers has nonetheless been able, thanks to improved agricultural techniques, to make France one of the world's leading agricultural exporters. In urban areas, the number of unskilled workers fell drastically from 1940 to the 1990s, replaced by more white-collar employees.

Given the economic prosperity during the last half of the century, most French came to take for granted things like cars and vacations in foreign countries, previously considered luxuries for the wealthy. A smaller percentage of the average French income was spent on basic necessities—food and lodging—than had been the case earlier in the century. Not only did salaries rise, but food also became cheaper due to increased production and to vast improvements in highways that lowered the cost of transporting goods. Consequently, many of the items the French purchase today are no longer produced in the area where they live. Local markets have largely melded into the national and European economies and now, in a development alarming to some French, into the global economy.

The move toward larger markets did not happen by chance. The European Union was established in 1957, not only to stimulate tariff-free trade among all member countries, but also, essentially, to promote long-term reconciliation of France and Germany. The founders of the European Union were all too aware of the dismal history of relations between France and Germany. Between 1870 and 1945, France had fought three wars against Germany. Each war seemed to create the conditions of possibility—or inevitability—for the next. The goal was to stop the vicious cycle. It worked. The French no longer live under the threat of war with Germany.

A photo appearing in a magazine showing French deportees leaving Fribourg, Germany to return to France. Behind them are German soldiers who have been taken prisoner.

The Vicious Cycle: Three Wars and Their Effects

From 1870 to the First World War

Many French people who lived through or fought in the war of 1870 against Prussia were ashamed to have been so soundly defeated, and to have lost the Alsace and Lorraine regions on their eastern border. For years the French army prepared to fight the *next* war against Germany that most military thinkers considered inevitable. (References to this inevitable conflict can even be found in pre-war school textbooks!) When war finally came in August 1914, French soldiers marched confidently off to meet the invaders. But their confidence soon gave way to dismay and even despair as German troops rolled into northern and eastern France and began to approach Paris. The French army recovered and held off the invaders, but it was already clear that this would be no short and glorious campaign, but a long and terrible ordeal. The armistice signed in 1918 restored honor to the French army and Alsace and Lorraine to France, but a terrible price was paid.

The Great War—*la grande guerre*, as it is still known in France—was a disaster for most Western countries; but the French suffered more than anyone else, including the defeated Germans. One out of six French soldiers died—nearly one and one-half million, or more than ten percent of the working population—and almost as many more were crippled, physically or spiritually (or both). Peasants paid a particularly heavy price; they constituted well over two-thirds of the total dead, and even the smallest French village has a *monument aux morts* that lists an appalling number of victims, often several from the same family. Among the effects of these losses was a serious decline in birth rates during the 1920s and 1930s; this decline reduced the number of teachers available later on to educate the children born in the post-war "baby boom." In addition, more than 600,000 women were widowed, and more than 700,000 children grew up without fathers.

Moreover, it must not be forgotten that the First World War was fought mainly on French soil. The damage was calculated at 55 billion francs—more than double France's total national product in the year before the war started. In addition, financing the war increased the national debt from 32 billion francs to 170 billion francs, imposing a heavy burden on the treasury and requiring increased taxes. Everywhere, housing and factories had to be rebuilt; bridges, roads, and railways repaired; and farmlands reclaimed. There was precious little money or labor left to do all these things. Little wonder, then, that after the armistice in 1918, the French insisted that Germany pay large reparations to compensate them for the destruction of their country—reparations that were for the most part never paid.

Another result of the First World War was that French military thinkers—led by Marshal Pétain, who had won a famous if very costly victory at Verdun—abandoned their predecessors' commitment to all-out offensive and concentrated on a defensive strategy. This turnaround was symbolized by the famous "Maginot line" of fortifications along France's border with Germany. Unfortunately, this strategy also led to France's being unprepared to fight a war that involved rapid, motorized troop and armored movements, air attacks, and communications by radio; on the eve of World War II, French commanders were still relying on messengers and even carrier pigeons to deliver their orders. The exclusive focus on defense also reflected strong pacifist feelings among the French population and its politicians; hardly anyone wanted to fight another war, or even to prepare for one.

Armistice, November 11, 1918. In 1940 Hitler required that the French sign their agreement—ceding control of northern France to the Germans—in the same train car.

1914-1918

1939-1945

After the First World War—"the war to end all wars"—most communities in France erected veterans' memorials. After World War II and then after the Algerian War, more names were added, sometimes etched into places not intended for that use.

A monthly magazine that covered the war. This issue, showing the variety of military forces allied to France, is dated August 15, 1915.

LA ROSE DE FRANCE

Political cartoons were very popular during the First World War. This drawing depicts Germany as a caterpillar inching across the French provinces, whose names adorn the rose petals (March, 1915).

World War II and the Occupation

The Nazis began preparing for war almost as soon as they came to power in Germany. In May 1940, their powerful modern army dashed around the northern flank of the Maginot line and quickly crushed the French forces. On June 20, the French government signed an armistice that gave the Germans direct control of the northern part of the country, leaving the southern part under the control of a regime headed by the aged Marshal Pétain and located in the small resort town of Vichy. The Vichy regime was never truly independent, and this fact became increasingly evident. Almost immediately, clandestine resistance groups were formed—the famous *maquis*—and began to sabotage German operations, to provide Allied forces with information, and to stage isolated attacks on German troops. General De Gaulle rallied French forces outside France and was in contact with resistance groups operating within France. With the help of resistance fighters like Jean Moulin—tortured and assassinated by the Gestapo in 1942 as he was unifying the three largest resistance groups—a sizeable French fighting unit was put together that participated in the final battles of the war.

Casualties and material damage were much more limited than they had been in the First World War, but the country had to deal with the agony and ambiguities of occupation. Early on, it may have seemed to many French people that the German victory was definitive and that they simply had to adapt to it. In any case, many French passively accepted German domination, and some enthusiastically collaborated with the Nazis.

French Resistance fighters on the Rue to Rivoli (across from the Louvre and Tuileries gardens).

In October 1940, the Vichy government, under no pressure from the Nazis, severely restricted the rights of French Jewish citizens. Henceforth Jews were not allowed to hold public office, work in the press in any capacity, teach on any level, or be involved in cultural activities. By July 1944, more than seventy thousand Jews had been deported (of which at least ten thousand were children). Less than 2,500 returned to France at the end of the war.

The French have gone through a long process of reflection regarding their activities during the war. In the immediate aftermath of the war, the French wanted to believe that more individuals were involved in the French Resistance than was, in fact, the case. René Clément's 1946 film, "Le père tranquille," for instance, tells the tale of an ordinary citizen who seems outwardly to be a collaborator but is in fact the head of the local Resistance. Almost thirty years later another film, Louis Malle's "Lacombe Lucien, " dealt with the war more harshly, raising the buried question of widespread collaboration. In 1987, Malle wrote and directed another poignant film, "Au Revoir les Enfants," based on his own reminiscence of a Jewish schoolmate who was denounced and deported. Painful as it was, the French came to speak openly of this, the darkest aspect of their collaboration.

Films, novels, and historical studies have, over the years, reflected and contributed to the French collective conscience about collaboration, as well as French participation in the Final Solution. They have led to several public acts of repentance and condemnation (for example, the Catholic Church's acknowledgement of guilt in a declaration of 1997, and the long overdue condemnations of collaborators, like a former secretary-general of

German officers stationed in Paris at the time of the liberation (August, 1944).

The 28th U.S. Infantry Division parades down the Champs Elysées on August 29, 1944. This was not only to celebrate the liberation of Paris, but also to move the troops toward combat positions in the east. They entered into active combat less than 24 hours after the parade in Paris.

Bordeaux, Maurice Papon, recently found guilty for having deported 1,690 Jews.) Slowly but surely, the French are including in historical and educational materials evidence that incriminates their own countrymen. Such is the case at the Invalides Museum in Paris where, in an exhibition on military history, there are photographs of French officials herding Jews onto trains bound for Auschwitz. The head of the museum, General Bernard Devaux, explained that it took so long (until the year 2000) because "the scars and wounds of the past were just too unhealed before."

French Literature

It must be recalled that despite the terrible suffering that the French endured in the first half of the twentieth century, this was also a time of enormous vitality in literature, art, and music. Paris was the undisputed cultural capital of the world for many years. The young expatriate writers trying to eke out a living there in the 1920s were dubbed by Gertrude Stein "the lost generation"—a term later used by Ernest Hemingway in "the Sun Also Rises" (1926) to describe the disillusioned young men living a hard-drinking existence in post-war Paris. They were "lost," like many of their French counterparts, in the sense that the moral values that they had inherited seemed meaningless after the devastation of the First World War.

Other French writers, especially those writing in the early 1930s, were impatient with the individualism of the "lost generation" and yearned for action. For instance, André Malraux filled his novels with adventure and fraternity, as well as a strong sense of political commitment. His *La Condition humaine (The Human Condition*, 1933) depicts the Communist uprising in Shanghai in 1927 and the young revolutionaries who fight to bring it about. In *L'espoir (Man's Hope*, 1937), Malraux describes the Spanish Civil War and the Republican fighters who fought a losing battle against the fascist General Franco. Malraux was a man of letters and a man of action. During the war, he commanded a group of underground resistance fighters; and after the war, he served as a minister in the Fifth Republic.

Not all politically committed writers were located on the left end the ideological spectrum. Drieu la Rochelle, for instance, writes about a young man who, after suffering a kind of mental and moral depression, decides to go to Spain and fight *with* Franco. Other French writers on the political right—Brasillach, Céline, and Rebatet—gave vent to their anti-Semitic feelings both in their fiction and in articles published during the Occupation.

For many French writers, however, being published was not an easy matter during the Occupation, though there was a clandestine press (the newspaper *Combat* and the book publishing house of Editions de Minuit). The works of some writers, such as the poets Paul Eluard and Louis Aragon, were transmitted orally; and some plays were able to be staged only because their "message" was camouflaged to get past the German censors. This was the case of Jean-Paul Sartre's *Les Mouches (The Flies*, 1943) and *Huis Clos (No Exit*, 1944).

After the war, writers like Sartre and Albert Camus, who had been politically committed and associated with the Resistance, achieved great popularity. By the 1950s, however, the intellectual scene was once again as diverse and divisive as ever. Writers and artists were attracted to different political and philosophical camps—Sartre and Camus, for example, ended their friendship—and a new generation of disillusioned youth opted to stay out of politics altogether. Simone de Beauvoir's novel, *Les Mandarins* (1954), describes the difficulty that French intellectuals experienced in trying to break out of the educated elite in order to engage in political activism. The novel also depicts two mutually exclusive poles of attraction for French intellectuals: Communism and the United States.

The End of French Colonialism

The Second World War changed the relationship of France to many of its overseas colonies. Colonies had provided the Free French movement with needed resources and, after the Allied victory, they demanded a change in their status: greater autonomy or complete independence from France. The French were still struggling with the loss of face that their quick defeat in 1940 by the Germans had caused. Could they handle the loss of their role overseas? Many government officials thought not. Mild concessions were granted in 1946, but they did not go far enough to satisfy the increasingly radical elements in the colonies.

Also in 1946, negotiations between the French and the Vietnamese nationalist movement led by Ho Chi Minh broke down, resulting in an eight-year war in Indochina.

The defeat suffered in the battle of Dien Bien Phu (Vietnam) in 1954 was a serious blow to French pride. Six months after the

French departure from Vietnam, a revolt against French rule broke out in Algeria. Although almost half a million French troops were sent to put it down, by 1958 things had reached a crisis point. Dismayed by the likelihood of defeat, right-wing and military forces began to plot the overthrow of the Fourth Republic, threatening to plunge the country into civil war. When, on May 13, 1958, a new cabinet was on the verge of presenting its program to the National Assembly, Algerian revolutionaries took control of Algiers. It seemed that there were only two viable solutions to the dilemma: either accept a coup d'État by the French army, or ask Charles De Gaulle to take charge of the government. On June 1 of that year, the National Assembly gave full power to De Gaulle for a period of six months. This act, in essence, ended the Fourth Republic.

De Gaulle seemed to begin his mandate with the belief that Algeria must remain French; but as time went by, he moved to a more moderate conciliatory position that would allow Algeria a good deal of autonomy while maintaining links to France. He was opposed by the most vociferous of Algerian nationalist leaders, and by the French, many of whom felt betrayed by his support of compromise. In 1961, a group of French army officers attempted a coup in Algiers. When it failed, the group became involved in terrorist activities. De Gaulle nonetheless ushered through a settlement that was approved by French voters. As a result, nearly a million French colonists left their homes in Algeria and headed to France. Referred to as "pieds noirs" (black feet), many of these French citizens had lived for generations in North Africa and had few ties to the mainland.

The decolonization of Algeria served as a catalyst, and other French territories in Africa soon demanded and were granted independence. The French government, rather than fighting the movements, decided to offer economic and military support in order to establish a French-speaking bloc of countries, thereby contributing to France's role as a world power.

The Events of May 1968

After the turmoil of the Vietnamese and Algerian crises, the 1960s seemed prosperous and peaceful . . . at least until 1968. On May 3, a minor student protest in Paris escalated into a major civil conflict involving not only students but workers as well. In the following two weeks, universities across the country joined the protest, and millions of workers went on strike. France was paralyzed. It seemed clear that the radical protestors were intent on bringing down the Fifth Republic.

As street violence escalated, the Communists refused to resort to force, and withdrew their support of the more radical factions. De Gaulle took advantage of this schism and dissolved the National Assembly, calling for votes on June 23 and 30. The Fifth Republic was maintained; the street barricades were dismantled; and life more or less returned to normal.

However, the unrest produced long-term effects: higher education was reformed in order to make it more democratic; workers' wages and working conditions were improved; and the women's movement was strengthened. The events of May 1968 also served to reinforce a kind of conservatism, as evidenced in the overwhelming support De Gaulle was accorded in a plebiscite held a month later. Most French who lived through the events

Here, the Eiffel Tower (1889) is viewed from the Centre Pompidou (1977). Both edifices shocked the public when they were erected, but both are now accepted by most French people and visited by thousands of tourists each year.

have vivid recollections of the extent of the social upheaval, and strong opinions as to whether the protests were warranted.

Two French Statesmen

Charles De Gaulle (1890–1970)

De Gaulle dominated the French political scene for half a century, even during years when he was not in office. He was a towering figure, in all senses of the word. His biographer, Jean Lacouture, recounts an episode that shows the extent of De Gaulle's sense of destiny and his hubris. When he was student at the War College, a friend told him that he had a strange feeling that he [De Gaulle] "would become great." Rather than laugh off the comment, as most young men might, De Gaulle reflected for a moment and then answered, "Yes, so do I."

Charles De Gaulle chose to pursue a military career, though his upper-middle-class family were more intellectuals than soldiers. As a young man, Charles fought in the First World War. He was wounded three times, taken prisoner, and tried to escape repeatedly. After the war, he became the protégé of Marshal Pétain and served in the French army occupying the Rhineland. During this time (1927–29), he wrote a study on the German military in which he exposed what he saw as the woeful inadequacy of the current French defense system: a static line along the border. He was convinced that tanks and other mobile armored vehicles would play a major offensive role in any future conflict with Germany, but he was unable to convince his superiors in the

French army. Of course, he was proved right when German *Panzer* divisions, supported by aircraft and motorized troops, staged a lightning attack through Belgium in 1940.

When Pétain was seeking an armistice with the Germans and forming the Vichy government, De Gaulle decided not to follow his former mentor. He travelled instead to England, where he issued his famous call to arms on the radio in order to convince the French to follow his lead and resist the Germans (June 18, 1940).

In England, De Gaulle worked against tremendous odds: he was not the head of an existing army, and had only a few followers. In August 1940, the French army court-martialed him in absentia, and sentenced to death for treason for having refused to serve under Pétain. Furthermore, his relations with Allied leaders were less than ideal. Archives reveal that his uncompromising and often truculent French nationalism annoyed Churchill and Roosevelt. Roosevelt, in fact, preferred to deal with the Vichy regime during most of the war.

Slowly, however, many French and Allies put their faith in De Gaulle. He was accepted by various resistance groups within France, whose acts of sabotage against the German occupiers he directed when communication was possible. By 1943 De Gaulle had established himself as the leader not only of the internal resistance and the "Free French Forces," but also as a major political figure who would play an important role in the future of France. In 1944 he and his "government" returned triumphantly to Paris, where he marched down the Champs-Élysées amidst the supportive cheers of Parisians, despite continuing sniper fire! Photos from this triumphant parade across Paris to Notre Dame Cathedral show that de Gaulle did not flinch or duck for cover as

A family shields itself from sniper fire during the liberation festivities in Paris, August 26, 1944.

General de Gaulle walked in a procession from the Arch of Triumph to Notre Dame. As the mass was celebrated, gunfire was still being heard (August 26, 1944).

the isolated gunshots rang out, as did many in his entourage. (Dying young was not part of his plan.)

As expected, De Gaulle became immediately involved in national politics, heading two provisional governments; but this came to an abrupt stop in 1946, when he resigned in protest against what he saw as a return of the partisan political maneuvering that had characterized the Third Republic. De Gaulle remained a vocal critic of the Fourth Republic until 1958, holding no office though he organized a kind of mass movement with enough weight to win 120 seats in the National Assembly in 1951. De Gaulle was still a powerful force in the country.

Ironically, it was the revolt of the French colonies, in which De Gaulle had found much needed support during the war, that led to his return to power. De Gaulle wrote a new constitution for the Fifth Republic, similar to the one he had proposed in 1945, creating a presidency with great executive powers, to which he was subsequently elected.

De Gaulle ruled the country as he had ruled the battlefield. His methods were often autocratic and paternalistic; since 1940, he had seen himself as the very embodiment of France, and was convinced he knew what was best for his country. His goal was to restore France's position as a world power, while maintaining its national independence (and especially its independence from American influence). To accomplish this goal, he relied on the strong presidency he had created and on his strong personality. In 1962 he gave the French a choice: his resignation or the acceptance of true universal suffrage for the presidential election (rather than election by an electoral college). The voters overwhelmingly supported him; he was elected in 1962 and again in

1965. During his terms as president, De Gaulle set about to modernize France. Under his leadership, France incontestably made great strides forward, becoming once again a major European power both economically and militarily.

The events of 1968 put De Gaulle to a new kind of test. The civil unrest of those months was unlike the international conflicts for which his military training had prepared him and his personality had disposed him. Although the voters ended up supporting his government, as opposed to backing the protesters, the support expressed more a desire for a return to normalcy than a vote of confidence for the president. Many felt that in the midst of the turmoil De Gaulle had been slow to act, letting his prime minister, Georges Pompidou, take the lead. In any case, the following year, De Gaulle put a referendum before the voters. Once again, he vowed to resign if it did not pass. Some commentators contend that there was little chance of the measure passing, leading them to conclude that De Gaulle was looking for an excuse to step down from office.

Charles De Gaulle resigned in April 1969, and spent the remaining eighteen months of his life writing. He was a writer of considerable merit whose work had been published since the 1920s. His enduring place in the pantheon of French literature was ensured especially by his memoirs.

François Mitterrand (1916–1996)

In many respects, François Mitterrand's political history seems the opposite of De Gaulle's. Mitterrand moved from the right to the left, whereas De Gaulle initially held a number of "leftist"

A sense of alienation followed the student revolts of 1968. This graffiti from the early 1970s also shows the use of English in expressions of protest, a use that has increased along with the spread of English in business and diplomacy across Europe.

views early in his career, but ended up in the center-right. Mitterrand worked for two governments that De Gaulle spurned: first Vichy and then, after the war, the Fourth Republic. During the dozen years that Mitterrand served the Fourth Republic, De Gaulle was an outspoken critic of it. When De Gaulle returned to power in 1958, it was Mitterrand who galvanized the opposition to him.

By 1965 Mitterand managed to make such a strong showing in the presidential election that De Gaulle was forced into a run-off election. In this election, as well as the two following, Mitterrand led the Socialist Party and had the French Communist Party's support. In 1974 Mitterrand ran against Valéry Giscard d'Estaing, and received ten percent more votes than the victor in the first round. Mitterand subsequently lost the election only because the center voted for Giscard on the second round. Mitterrand continued to lead the opposition through Giscard's seven years in the presidency; and, in the 1981 elections, a coalition among the various leftist parties brought about Mitterrand's surprising victory. He held the presidency from 1981–1995.

Much has been written about Mitterrand's years as president. For all the positive programs and changes put into effect—raising the minimum wage, increasing social benefits, abolishing the death penalty, and improving relations with the United States—many people on the left became disenchanted with their leader. By the end of his first term (1981–1988), government policies were no longer undertaken in the spirit of socialism but rather according to principles of free-market liberalism. Many felt that Mitterrand had abandoned the left.

In foreign policy, Mitterrand was an enthusiastic supporter of a more unified Europe; he was one of the drafters of the Maastricht

A village grocery store in the 1970s. Many such stores have been forced to close their doors, unable to compete with large supermarkets to which most people can now drive.

An open market in the 1980s. Some vendors at open markets now fear that new European legislation concerning refrigeration might drive them out of business.

Treaty that sought to strengthen the structure of the European Community. In 1991, he called for a popular referendum in France to support the treaty, and received a mere 51% in support. Clearly, he had hoped for more. The high rate of unemployment in France— 12% by 1993—undoubtedly contributed to wariness on the part of the French toward a more economically unified Europe.

To make matters worse, a series of financial scandals beset the Socialists; a prime minister was forced to resign and then committed suicide. The Socialists were soundly defeated in the parliamentary elections of 1993. This electoral upset caused Mitterrand to take on, for the second time in his presidency, a prime minister from the opposition. Although this "cohabitation," as it is called in French, can provide a check-and-balance system, it can also lead to frequent stalemates. During his last two years in office, Mitterrand was forced to work with a center-right prime minister, Edouard Balladur.

In 1996, Mitterrand died from cancer. His fifteen-year battle with the disease had been a closely guarded secret.

Immigration and Social Tensions

In the early part of the twentieth century, France had the reputation of being very open to immigration. One reason is obvious: after the devastation of the First World War, France desperately needed manpower. In the inter-war period, three million people immigrated to France, mostly from neighboring countries: Italians (35%), Poles (20%), Spanish (15%), and Belgians (10%). Likewise, there was a labor shortage after World War II, though this need was caused more by economic expansion than by war casualties. Up to the 1960s, immigration accounted for 40% of the growth of the French population. Immigration slowed in the 1970s, but there were nonetheless some four million foreigners living in France by the 1980s. By this time, however, fewer immigrants came from Europe and more from North Africa.

North African immigrants—Algerians, Moroccans, and Tunisians—were often males who came as low-skilled workers, lived together in low-income housing, and sent money home to their families. This situation slowly changed in the 1980s as North African families were gradually united and new families arrived together. There thus arose a sizeable population of children born in France to foreign-born parents. During times when the economy was at low ebb, the government repeatedly tried to restrict both immigration and the naturalization of immigrants' children. For the most part, however, immigration continued unabated and young people born in France of non-French parents were granted citizenship upon request. In the 1990s, immigrants made up between five and ten percent of the overall population. Many foreign workers accepted jobs that French citizens disdained: monotonous factory work, street and metro cleaning, etc.

Throughout the latter half of the century, and especially at times of high unemployment, immigrants were often targets of discrimination. The leader of one far-right party, Jean-Marie Le Pen, popularized the slogan, "La France aux Français" ("France for the French") in his anti-immigrant speeches; and even the leader of French Communists, Georges Marchais, once threatened to bulldoze the homes of immigrant workers.

Even Le Pen would probably acknowledge that it is abusive to regard the French as a race. As we saw in our first chapter, the population of what we today call France comprises a wide assortment of peoples who arrived over thousands of years from distant lands. The people living in France today reflect that mixture. What a French person might see as his or her link to another French person, besides the resemblance of their passports, is less their common racial attributes than their shared participation in French *culture*.

Although most French would be hard put to define what French culture is, they think they can say what it *is not*. French culture is not North African and not Islamic. The resentment against North African immigrants seems based less on their racial differences than on cultural differences. Once in France, many North Africans maintain their religious and cultural practices, living together in closely-knit neighborhoods, wearing traditional dress (especially the women), and speaking Arabic—a language not widely taught in French schools. For over thirty years, a sizeable North African community has existed in France; but the rate of integration of these people and their children into upper-level skilled jobs has been considerably slower than it was for the European immigrants who came to France in the first half of the century. The census report of 1999 concludes that, for the over two million working immigrants in the country, the risk of unemployment was greater than for French individuals with equivalent qualifications. The inclusion of immigrant women into the work force remains similarly difficult.

Education

The great strides made in public education in the nineteenth century are apparent as the third millennium begins; literacy is close to 100% in France. Virtually all children that reside in France attend school, which is free and compulsory up to the age of sixteen. Even private schools—for the most part Catholic—follow an academic curriculum administered nationally, though individual schools and teachers have a free hand in choosing their own materials and methodologies. In theory, children in the same grade level are all learning the same things, regardless of where they live in France.

The goal of uniformity in quality is harder to achieve than uniformity in content. Urban schools are often at an advantage over small rural schools that must place several grades in one classroom; and schools in affluent areas have an advantage over those located in low-income areas, such as predominantly immigrant neighborhoods. One can detect a kind of "brain drain" caused by veteran teachers requesting transfers to schools with better reputations and fewer discipline problems. Also undermining the republican ideal of equality in education is a current trend in which parents move their children to better schools, either by requesting a transfer from their local mayor or by purchasing or renting a home in the desired school district.

Despite these problems, France can rightly boast of its high-caliber educational system at the primary and secondary levels. French lycées (high schools) were established by Napoleon in 1801 in order to educate the elite of France. This aspect of the French lycée did not change until after World War II, when a process of democratization began. In 1946 a mere four percent of the population attained the *baccalauréat*, the degree conferred upon passing an examination at the end of lycée study. By 1999 that figure had risen to 60%.

In higher education, France has two parallel systems: the regular university that is administered by the government, free of charge, and open to any student with a *baccalauréat*; and the *grandes écoles*, prestigious institutes to which admission is granted on the basis of a test given after the *baccalauréat*. (*Grandes écoles* admit only a very small percentage of those who apply.) Once admitted to a university, a student completes a year or two of general study, and then has to pass another examination before continuing to higher, more specialized study. In contrast to universities in the United States, French schools of higher learning are hardly distinguishable from one another, because of the uniformity in curriculum throughout the country. If many college students flock to Paris, it is more because of what the capital has to offer culturally than because of the superiority of the universities there.

As the twentieth century closed and the national unemployment figures remained stubbornly in two digits, debate continued as to the role of secondary schools and universities in preparing students to join the workforce. Should they be redesigned to offer more professional guidance and training? It appears probable that in the coming decades, French education will develop in new directions that take into account the economic and demographic changes the country has undergone.

Epilogue

We would be naïve, however, to imagine that France will quickly or radically change their educational system, or any other aspect of their society. The French continue to display a pervasive respect for their history and their institutions, even when they vociferously criticize them. The most recent photograph in this book, taken in the first months of the third millennium, shows a shepherd with his flock. His gesticulating hand expresses the passion that he feels as he condemns the progressive industrialization of sheep raising in France. Nevertheless, the fact remains that he, and others like him, are still here, leading their sheep from one pasture to another.

A shepherd at the turn of the century (19ᵗʰ to 20ᵗʰ century)

A shepherd at the turn of the century (20ᵗʰ to 21ˢᵗ century)

INDEX

Illustrations are noted in italics.